DEVELOPING STRATEGIC ALLIANCES

★★★★★★

Ed Rigsbee

Developing Strategic Alliances
Ed Rigsbee

CREDITS:
Editor: George Young, Barbara Atmore
Design and Production: Fifth Street Design

© 2000 Crisp Publications, Inc., Menlo Park, CA 94025

Printed in the United States of America by Von Hoffmann Graphics

www.crisplearning.com

04   10 9 8 7 6 5 4 3 2

Library of Congress Catalog Card Number 99-75058

Rigsbee, Ed
Developing Strategic Alliances

ISBN 1-56052-550-9

Introduction

Partnering is the *modus operandi* of the third millennium. This book will help you develop your own systematic process for building successful strategic partnering alliances. The word *alliance* conjures up a multitude of meanings based on your personal experience. It could bring to mind positive, or negative feelings. Partnering, unfortunately, is the most mis-used and abused term in business today. Through using this book, you will learn how to profit from the partnering trend. You will learn how to formulate strategic alliances that work for you.

An alliance can have many degrees of formality. An alliance can be simply a handshake agreement between two people to help each other whenever possible. An alliance can be an agreement between two local business people agreeing to advertise together. An alliance can also be a contractual agreement between two businesses for distribution, R&D, or cross promotions, or an alliance can be a joint venture between two or more large corporations to develop, manufacture, and distribute a new product. An alliance can even be between countries as with the North Atlantic Treaty Organization (NATO) for mutual protection from aggres-sors. Regardless of the level of your strategic alliance, many of the cru-cial success elements remain the same.

In this book, I offer solid ideas on how to develop your own strategic alliances successfully. You must select your alliance partner well and then intelligently develop the framework. Once your alliance is going, you must work hard to keep it alive and healthy. This book will help you to do all of the above. Additionally, in Appendix A you will find value-added checklists from The Corporate Partnering Institute. These checklists will help you keep yourself out of alliance quicksand. Let's face it, you've heard your fair share of partnering horror stories, we all have. Take to heart the ideas offered in this book and you'll be glad you did.

In the final analysis, what you really want is to build **Outrageously Successful Relationships (OSRs)** with people. Building OSRs is easy to understand but difficult in the execution. Why? We're all in such a hurry these days that we do not always take time to understand the needs of others. In our new world of high-tech, we forget the crucial need every human being has for high-touch. Building OSRs could be seen as a "soft" skill but it isn't—building OSRs can have an important impact on the bottom-line profitability of your enterprise. The better your relation-ship is with your alliance partner, the better you will be able to blend your core competencies. Coupling your core competency with your alliance partner's core competency delivers a synergy to your alliance, and that's what partnering is all about.

Many of the ideas in this book grew from my previous book titled, *The Art of the Partnering*. In *The Art of Partnering*, I presented my model for Total Organizational Partnering. The model is called the Pentad Partnering —five areas in which every business should develop partnering activities through a partnering mind set. The five areas: Strategic Alliances, Alliances with Suppliers, Alliances with Customers, Alliances with Employees, and You, the executive or business owner becoming the Optimal Partner.

A five leg star was the graphic I used in *The Art of Partnering* to make the point. In my seminars across North America, I would explain each leg of the star and then ask attendees what went in the middle—it's the idea of relationships. Relationships are the foundation of how business is conducted. Who you choose to buy your daily bread from, where you take your clothes to be laundered, and what restaurants you enjoy are all based on relationships. It's no different in your business. If you build **OSRs** in all five areas of your business, regardless of your size, you will be successful at Total Organizational Partnering. To be on top with your profitability, you must have TOP (Total Organizational Partnering).

While alliances are not for everybody, they might be right for you. Alliance relationships are for the mature. If you want to optimize your chances for alliance success, you must have an **Emotional Ownership** in the idea. In Chapter 6 you will find ideas on how to have an emotional ownership of the idea of alliance relationships. You will also find a chart showing you the path. All of the ideas in this book are only useful if you do have, or find, your personal *Emotional Ownership* of the idea of strategic alliances.

Throughout the book, you will find examples of strategic alliances, both with large and small businesses. If you are a small business, or an independent supplier of goods or service, the key is to take the idea and adapt it to your situation. If you're a small business person, do not get caught in the immobility trap by saying, "This only works for the big boys." Change is the hallmark of today's business environment. So, change and shift based both on your own business needs and the needs of your market. Please, do not be afraid to give alliance relationships a try. I hope you receive the value from this book that I know is possible for you. Call my office (800) 839-1520 or visit my web site **www.rigsbee.com** if you have an alliance or a business relationship problem you can't solve and maybe together we can create some solution synergy. I wish you the best of success in building relationship bridges that serve you and your alliance partner(s).

Ed Rigsbee
Westlake Village, California
June 1999

Chapter 1

★★★★★★★

What's In It For Me?

★★★★★★

"Almost all of our relationships begin and most of them continue as forms of mutual exploitation, a mental or physical barter, to be terminated when one or both parties run out of goods."

— W.H. Auden, 1962

Reasons and Benefits of Developing Strategic Alliances

The reasons for strategic alliances become apparent when you understand the benefits. This applies to businesses and organizations of all sizes. Your reason for developing an alliance could be for research, production, marketing, distribution, or management. Your increased capability for success through alliance relationships will encourage your continued embracing of the practice. The same holds true regardless of whether you enter strategic alliances as an individual or as an organization. Many of the benefits create high value for different segments of the distribution chain rather than all the segments.

I'm not going to specifically tell you which benefits relate to manufacturers, wholesale distributors, retailers and service organizations. The reason is that I do not want you to limit yourself. Innovation can be creating a new wheel or adapting another's idea to your situation. What's in it for you? Maybe all of the benefits listed below, or maybe only a few. How much benefit you receive will be a function of your self-imposed limits, (or hopefully a lack them).

In developing your strategic alliances, you are only limited by the quality of your alliance relationships and your imagination!

There are seven general areas in which you can profit from building alliances:

1. Products
2. Access
3. Operations
4. Technology
5. Strategic Growth
6. Organization
7. Finance

Your basic strengths may lead you to develop alliances in only a few areas, or you may desire to develop alliances in many areas over time. Work hard to develop the **Outrageously Successful Relationships (OSRs)** in all your alliances. You will discover *what's in it for you*, if you develop the right alliance, with the right people. What follows are some of the options.

Technological Sophistication

- *An exchange of technology.* Compliment your basic strengths, shore up your weakness, and improve production capabilities to better serve customers. An example of this type of alliance is the one between Kinko's Service Corp. of Ventura (copy centers) and Xerox Engineering Systems to establish a nationwide network for faxing large-format documents. This service is especially valuable to architects, contractors, and advertising agencies. Kinko's gets a revenue boost and Xerox gets additional placement and unit sales.

- *Technical hotlines and on-site technical support.* These are regularly available from suppliers with whom you've developed alliances.

- *A technological contribution or possibly a technological edge in your industry.* The alliance between IBM and Apple to develop a new computer operating system that allows both hardware formats to communicate. Nynex Corp. and Philips Electronics joined to develop screen telephones for residential use. These alliances, especially involving technology, need not be permanent, only lasting as long as they are mutually beneficial.

Training

- *Learning curve commitment.* Cost savings are passed along as experience is gained in producing a new product, and discounts are available on start-up products to encourage early sales.

- *Better sales and technical training for your employees.* This is an important benefit in partnering with your suppliers. More manufacturers and distributors are developing training programs for dealers—Guggenheim Dental, a dental supply distributor in Hawthorne, CA, is now regularly offering training programs for their top customers. Recently, at a seminar I delivered for the National Nutritional Foods Association, I suggested to the retailers that they only buy their nutritional supplements from suppliers that offer training videos and materials. This is an added benefit in the seller/buyer relationship.

Increase Market Share

- ***Co-branding.*** Snack manufacturers are now mixing two nationally known names and logos on a single product. Examples of this are Betty Crocker's Soda-Licious, (soda pop fruit snacks), made with 7UP and 7UP Cherry and the popular milk chocolate-covered Pretzel Flipz by Nestlé featuring Rold Gold pretzels.

- ***Access to new markets.*** Both domestic and international may be available. Copeland Corporation joined with the largest compressor manufacturer in India, Kirloskar, to bring air conditioning to a growing middle class.

- ***Positioning for future needs.*** An early-adapting firm is one whose present needs will reflect its industry needs in future months or years. Through partnering, one company can assist another in leapfrogging current industry leaders. This is done by cooperating with newer firms more willing to pursue a riskier development strategy to gain market share. This strategy can aid companies, large and small, in more rapidly and efficiently reaching their collective goals.

- ***Additional business to justify operating a production facility.*** In developing strategic alliances with competitors, you might do the production for both. This is similar to retailers who have a store brand developed by the recognized national brand manufacturer.

- ***Opportunity to develop a private labeling or branding identity.*** American Dental Cooperative in St. Louis, MO has been successful in this area, as has Power Heavy Duty in the heavy duty truck repair industry.

- ***Sales leads and help in procuring new business.*** Brian Potts, a VP at 3M recently made an offer to his customers strategic building service contractors at their CEO retreat in Mexico. He pointed out how other 3M divisions are most likely selling to the customers that the contractors seek and how they could take advantage of those already established relationships.

- ***Opportunity to expand business using new or related product innovations and service offerings.*** (Later in the book you will find out how Helen Chavez at La Tapatia Tortilleria did this).

- **Preferred supplier status.** Steelcase in Grand Rapids, MI awards a designation as a preferred supplier to those who have proven their performance abilities.

- **Reduce direct competition.** The Sun/IBM alliance has attempted this in creating the Java operating system to keep Microsoft at bay.

- **To gain market share.** Coach, the New York-headquartered manufacturer of fine leather products, teamed up with Lexus in an exclusive partnership to produce the Limited Lexus ES 300 Coach Edition.

- **Geographic expansion.** Ronald Fink's West Palm Beach, FL company, RGF Environmental Group, found that new business expanded following a trip to Asia with other local CEOs and Ray Reddish, a senior management analyst at Florida's Commerce Department. Within 18 months of his trip, Reddish had hired 14 new employees just to handle his Pacific Rim business. Some states aggressively partner with local manufacturers to expand exporting there by increasing state revenue.

- **Create marketing synergism to the consumer through cross promotion.** Blockbuster and Dominoes Pizza created a promotion that required a customer to rent three movies, in return they received a $10 savings book for Dominoes Pizza. Both partners received increased traffic through the joint promotion. This is often more easily done at the local level between, as an example, a drug store and a dry cleaner.

- **Barriers to market entry by a new player.** This protects the current players as with GTE and Pacific Bell in Los Angeles. They partnered to serve UCLA in a method that closed an opportunity to a new provider attempting to enter their market.

- **Marketing assistance to support order volume for product.** This can happen when a small company develops an alliance with a large company who can assist with manufacturing, fulfillment, or distribution.

Improved Customer Service

- **Improved attitude toward customer service.** This starts best with support from top management. Many manufacturers are partnering with their dealers and retailers. When the dealer makes a long-term buying commitment to the manufacturer, the manufacturer helps the dealer with customer service tools and training.

- **Improved customer loyalty.** United Airlines developed this through their alliance with Starbucks. United now serves Starbucks' gourmet coffee to their passengers at 30,000 feet. And they do it in cups bearing the logos of both companies.

- **Improved product offering.** This can become possible through alliance buying cooperatives. Additional product lines become available to the members because of the cooperative's buying strength. This is an old method of cooperation that works.

Barnett Gershen, CEO of Associated Building Services in Houston, builds alliances with his customers through a quarterly review method. Once a quarter, he sits down with his customers and asks for a grade or score as to the quality of service his company delivered. He then looks for tactics and strategies to improve his service.

Through alliance relationships, many businesses have found strategies to provide better and quicker customer service while keeping their costs manageable. Look for companies that have a similar customer base to yours and enter into a discussion about how to work together.

Innovation

The computer and electronics industries have profited greatly from alliance relationships. Innovation has become commonplace for firms that have chosen to work together. The University of Toronto's Innovations Foundation signed an agreement with Northway Explorations Ltd. and Polyphalt, a private Ontario, Canada company, to deliver polymer-modified asphalt materials technology for longer lasting roads to the commercial market.

To differentiate oneself from the competition, Steelcase developed an alliance with Peerless Lighting, located in Berkeley, CA, to offer state-of-the-art office lighting. The relationship has brought Steelcase an additional $15 to $35 million in annual furniture sales. Also, they received additional dollars from the light fixture billings.

Cost Savings

- **In manufacturing.** Elements of your product or entire product that could be built in plants (owned by others or in joint venture) with up-to-date technology, cost savings can be great. Sharing resources, or outsourcing, rather than owning and operating a manufacturing plant, will allow a synergistic partnering agreement, allowing you to concentrate on your core strengths. This is the idea behind the Donnelly Corporation and its venture with Applied Films Laboratory, Inc. for manufacturing and supplying the world market in display coated glass for liquid crystal displays (LCDs).

- **In distribution.** Developing access to orders that can be economically and efficiently produced and delivered. Also generates reasonable profit through alliance relationships.

- **Shared locations.** Many banks across the country are adding branch offices in suburban supermarkets. They are saving resources while simplifying the lives of their consumers by reducing the amount of time their customers spend on daily errands. Wal-Mart has a partnering alliance with Ronald McDonald, in many recently completed Wal-Mart stores. Signs on the store's entrance doors proudly display *"McDonald's Inside"* and a life-size plastic Ronald who sits inside on a bench to greet customers. Stores within stores have become commonplace through alliance relationships.

Financial Stability

- Partnering in a poor economy or recession makes good sense, especially when sales are flat and prices are deflating. Continental Airlines accessed optical industry consumers by partnering with Swan Optical, Inc., an industry supplier, to increase business through an air travel discount certificate program for purchasers of optical frames supplied by Swan.

- Access to capital is a primary reason for smaller organizations to develop alliances with larger ones. An example on a huge scale occurred when Chrysler went to the Federal Government seeking loan guarantees. On a smaller scale, Bruce Bendoff, CEO of Craftsman Custom Fabricators, Inc., Schiller Park, IL, a 275-employee sheet-metal bending company, learned how to grow through trusting the corporate behemoth Motorola.

- Achieving economies of scale is possible in alliance relationships when partners share facilities, equipment, and employees.

- Prompt payment per agreed terms is a standard in customer/supplier alliance relationships.

- More potential profit is generally the outcropping of shared resources.

- Alliance relationships allow partners to share the financial risks associated with developing new products and entering into new markets.

Buying Parity with Giants

- Working together, American Dental Cooperative members, dental distributors, are successfully purchasing goods in parity with the two giants in their industry.
- Additional discounts and services for in-depth marketing and technical expertise. Win/win pricing becomes possible in long-term buyer/seller alliance relationships.

Supply Chain Improvements

Just-in-time inventory purchasing and supplying are a great boon to the bottom-line, as exemplified by the famous relationship between Wal-Mart and Proctor & Gamble. Home Depot and Dell Computers have also built powerful alliances with their suppliers for cost saving just-in-time inventory.

Additional supply chain improvement areas that can benefit strategic alliance relationships:

- Management of supply channel conflict
- On-time product delivery
- Prompt response to complaints
- Greater consistency in parts, supplies, semi-assembled, and completed products
- Detailed agreement as to handling of product problems and customer complaints
- Improved supply chain productivity
- Specific (quarterly, yearly, etc.) volume commitments
- Key contacts who are dedicated to your account
- Improved supplier loyalty
- Prompt response to quote requests and price problems
- Confidentiality of shared business strategy

Productivity Increases

- Productivity increases are also achieved through partnering alliances. In a three-year study of Brown & Root/Braun's alliance with Union Carbide Corp., Danbury, CT, B&R/B concluded from a review of 18 projects that productivity on partnering jobs was about 16% to 17% higher than previous levels.

- The Arizona and California Departments of Transportation have successfully discovered that the partnering approach benefits from the experience of many industries. For example, working with the construction industry, they eliminated the tangle of claims, litigation, and adversarial relationships by developing a concept of cooperation throughout the life of a project. Identifying potential relationship hazards early was another benefit. Benchmarking (companies sharing information on what they do best), especially in the aerospace industry, has shown increased productivity and decreased costs across the board.

- Putting some pleasure and fun back into business. Jim Eisenhart, president of Ventura Consulting Group, Inc., Ventura, CA, says that the big benefit of partnering lies in putting pleasure and fun back into the construction business. He says people are now open to partnering because they recognize the limits of the old adversarial paradigms.

Some additional productivity increases that can be achieved through strategic alliance relationships:

- Market intelligence relating to new products, processes, and competitive technologies and markets

- Market intelligence relating to new products, processes, and competitive technologies and markets

- Market forecasts for large orders to allow intelligent production schedules

- Improved product quality

- Improved working relationships

- Improved communications through structure to promote operating efficiencies

- Improvement of products/services

- Sharing of information
- Improved culture and business philosophy
- Recognition, award and/or reward system for meeting and/or exceeding established goals
- Reduced paperwork

Ultimately the benefit to developing strategic alliances with others is found in creating solutions through mutually beneficial efforts. Together you can solve your problems and those of your customers, suppliers, and employees. Be sure you know what it is that you want to get from each of your alliance efforts! It's rare that a company can be all things to all people. Working in cooperation with others is the ideal solution. Strategic alliances can often get you much closer to your goals than working toward them without these valuable relationships. Finally, and decisively important, when a company embraces the philosophy of strategic alliances the result will be improvement in quality, productivity, and profitability. And yes, this is done through cooperation and collaboration.

Chapter 2

★★★★★★

Types of Strategic Alliances

★★★★★★

"Togetherness, for me, means teamwork. It makes us reflect how completely dependent we are upon one another in our social and commercial life. The more diversified our labors and interests have become in the modern world, the more surely we need to integrate our efforts to justify our individual selves and our civilization."

—Walt Disney

A recent issue of *The Economist* stated, "Alliances now account for 18% of the revenues of America's biggest companies." Corning receives about 25% of its revenue from equity positions (alliances). Today there is a trend in big business to stick to core competence and let outsiders help in the areas that are not a core strength. Small business can take a lesson here. In small business the tendency is to do everything in-house, believing they can do it better, or cheaper, themselves. This erroneous belief takes small business away from their core strength and forces them to play in a sandbox where they are weak. One of the best reasons to build a strategic alliance is to allow your business to concentrate on what it knows rather than what it doesn't. Let's look at a few big company solutions.

Nestlé developed a distribution alliance with Coca-Cola. Coca-Cola is a supplier with McDonald's. McDonald's developed a co-branding alliance with Disney. Disney developed a supply alliance with Coca-Cola. (It can get confusing...) Actually there are as many transparent, or hidden, alliances as there are promoted alliances. In each case, the companies formed strategic relationships that created synergies for all that were involved. Doug Ivester, chairman at Coca-Cola, says that 100% of his company revenue comes from alliances—alliance bottlers, alliance distributors, and so on.

Coca-Cola is quickly becoming a model for large corporation alliance builders. In addition to what we have mentioned, they recently entered into a national alliance agreement with "The Culligan Man." Culligan will supply the water filtering service for all Coke fountain outlets since Culligan was the only company who had the international capability to deliver the necessary service. Coca-Cola has also entered into an agreement with the packaged ice industry to create more awareness in the minds of consumers. The possibilities are endless!

Silicon Graphics in Mountain View, CA, developed 3-D graphics computing. Their computers were used to generate the dinosaurs in the movie *Jurassic Park*. They have developed about a dozen formal strategic alliance relationships. Edward McCracken, Chairman and CEO, has been the driving force in building Silicon Graphics' strategic alliances that include moviemakers George Lucas and Steven Spielberg. Silicon Graphics also partnered with Nintendo of America in a high-stakes alliance to create the Nintendo 64 video game system. They do it right— they create synergies!

Synergy, simply put, is when the joined alliance equals more than the sum of its separate parts (1+1 = 3). Alliance relationships are similar to a marriage between a man and a woman. There is still *the man* and *the woman* and now there is a third entity, the joined *couple*. As long as all three entities give and receive value from the relationship (or strategic alliance), the chances of the relationship continuing are good. If any of the three entities discontinue receiving and giving value, the chances of the relationship continuing are not so good.

Alliance relationships run the spectrum from external to internal, from vendor transactions to mergers, acquisitions, and subsidiaries. Most of the focus in this book is in the external areas of joint ventures, equity partnerships, franchise alliances, strategic business partnering, and preferred suppliers. A 1994 alliance study of small business (annual revenues less than $50 million) by Securities Data Company in Newark, NJ yielded the following results as to the types of alliances developed:

- 26% Marketing
- 21% Joint Ventures
- 21% Research & Development
- 15% Manufacturing
- 13% Licensing
- 3% Minority Equity Stake
- 1% Funding

In Chapter 1 we looked at a "what's in it for you" viewpoint in developing strategic alliances. You probably came up with ideas about the types of strategic alliances you might want to develop. On the following pages, I've listed many of the types of alliances and some examples. Many have come from my research in preparation for my alliance keynote presentations and seminars that I deliver to national trade and professional associations on the subject of alliances.

Types of Strategic Alliances

Strategic Alliances for Marketing

Cross Promotion is a popular reason for companies coming together.

Ideas are as simple as a local pharmacy and dry cleaner promoting each other with specials or coupons. Businesses can create regional promotions or take part in national promotions. Almost everywhere you look, you can see one organization cross promoting with another. Recently, I found an advertisement in a San Francisco newspaper for Pacific Bell. Their cross promotion also involved Round Table Pizza, Hollywood Video, Nokia, and Special Olympics.

Researching for a presentation for the National Home Furnishings Association, I discovered an interesting alliance in Northern California. They call themselves the Sonoma County Fine Furniture Association (SCFFA). What did they do? Eight local fine furniture retailers, all of them competitors, banded together to survive the recession of the early 1990s through cross promotion and buying strength. They bought advertising together on the local radio and in the local newspaper. They even dictated to the newspaper on which pages their advertising would be located. They developed combined events where customers would visit several of the stores to be eligible to win prizes. They promoted each other to their customers within the store, especially if the specific retailer did not have exactly what the customer was seeking. They even printed a combined brochure, including the address and map locations of each member. The front of the brochure said: "People you can trust." Wow, what impact!

On a United Airlines flight from Washington, D.C. to Atlanta, the cabin attendant handed me my usual bag of peanuts. But what was unusual was the size of the bag and its weight. After closer examination, I noticed that an America Online (AOL) diskette was included with the peanuts. It made sense: a business route shuttle—what a great way to get the AOL software into the hands of businesspeople.

Strategic Alliances for Co-Branding are usually alliances of trusted names created to develop marketing power.

The advertisement headline read, "Bring The Magic of Mattel Home for the Holidays." Just under the headline, several food producing toys were offered. The hook was that it showed Golden Arches food, as Mattel had a relationship with McDonald's. And what parent would deny their child the opportunity to make their own McDonald's hamburgers, fries, shakes, and cookies at home?

Like the Nestlé/Rold Gold Pretzel Flip I mentioned earlier, the positive effect that can be developed by co-branding is awesome. Co-branded products have, at a minimum, twice the marketing impact and customer pull as traditional branding. Consumers believe that with two trusted names, the product must be exceptional. There was one problem with "the Flip" though: when it was first introduced, consumer acceptance was so great that the distributors had trouble keeping their stores in stock. What a problem to have!

Strategic Alliances to Serve National Customers can mean increased volume and profitability for your business.

Serving the national customers creates special value in that they usually supply a continued flow of jobs and revenue. These alliances range from joint ventures to loose cooperatives.

The building service contracting industry services large commercial, manufacturing, and office buildings. It generally supplies janitorial, snow removal, trash removal, recycling, light bulb replacement, pest control, and other such services on a contract basis. Two respected companies in the industry, FBG (Omaha, NE) and Varsity Contractors (Pocatello, ID) formed a joint venture in 1994. The venture, called Network Services Company, is responsible for managing a $12 million, six-year contract with U.S. West for about 2,000 buildings in eleven states. By working together, they can achieve the goal of the contract—an 18% reduction of cost in the first three years and a 50% improvement in customer satisfaction.

John Dicks, owner of Awnex in Woodstock, GA, found himself in an enviable position through attracting national accounts like McDonald's, but it created the challenge of delivering the service necessary to maintain the account. The industrial fabrics industry, or as most know it, canvas awnings, has experienced a bad rap over the years due to the unreliability of the smaller companies in service and quality.

After a failed attempt to open satellite locations, John Dicks took a new direction: he pulled together several other fabricators and formed a strategic alliance called Awnet. Awnet has divided the country into five regions. Members share national accounts with one another and do all the work for the national accounts that fall into their regions. This alliance serves the national customers well since they now have the required consistency of service and quality to offer nationally. The individual fabricators win because they don't have to try to open shops across the country, yet they still enjoy the regional business of several national customers.

Another group, World Sign Associates (WSA) in the Denver area, receives some of the same benefits form their alliance. Nationally, all of the WSA members are tops in their geographical area at building and installing electric and neon signs. They operate separately but frequently use each other's services in installing signs built by one member that must be installed by another member out of their geographic area.

I recently visited several of the WSA members' locations in preparation for a seminar I delivered at their annual meeting. The one thing that impressed me was their relationship with one another even though they are scattered across the country. I frequently heard members say that they could *trust* one another. How can you put a price on that benefit?

Industry-specific Geographical Strategic Alliances serve the customers of the alliance well.

A great example of this type of alliance is a group called The Minnesota Connection. They serve the direct marketing industry. Their greatest benefit in soliciting customers is their close proximity to one another and the completeness of their combined services. The alliance includes ACI Telemarketing, Plastic Products, Nahan Printing, Mackay Envelope (yes, it's Harvey's company), Gage Lettershop Services, and I.C. Systems (list processing). For direct marketers, they can do it all. The Minnesota Connection can fulfill all the needs of direct mail customers since they are only a few minutes' drive by car from one another. This saves shipments criss-crossing the country and getting lost. If a problem occurs, one service provider visits the other in person and gets it handled. What a great selling point when prospecting for new business and keeping loyal customers!

Community-based Alliances such as professionals and small businesses can foster new development.

Firms can reduce marketing costs by positioning themselves with a public activity and share in the expenses as well as the rewards. John Grace, President of Investors Advantage Corporation in Westlake Village, CA, in conjunction with others in the local business community, puts together an annual event called the Economic Forum. The forum is designed to set apart his business from his look-alike competitors. Grace's strategic alliance consists of a local CPA firm, a bank, a law firm, a newspaper, a university school of business, a commercial real estate brokerage firm, an insurance agent, and a restaurant. They host more than 200 clients and guests each year at their forum.

The forum, first held at the local university and now at the city's new civic center, boasts high-level speakers who discuss the major economic concerns of the community residents in attendance. One year, in a continuing endeavor to maintain uniqueness, the invitations were printed on the only paper in the world made from post-consumer U.S. currency.

The sponsoring firms enjoy excellent name recognition and the ability to cross-pollinate clients, and, show appreciation and guidance to existing clients. The forum produces goodwill in the community, receives leads from interested attendees, and conducts business. In fact, after hearing a cassette tape of the event and some limited discussion with a registered financial representative, one person gladly handed over an investment check of $100,000.

Alliances with Your Competition at the onset may appear to be a poorly devised strategy at best, possibly even a strategy born in desperation.

If you approach this proposition without adopting the partnering principles talked about earlier, you could end up holding a tiger by the tail and wondering what in the world to do with it.

Andy Cowart, owner of Cowart and Company Inc. in Lexington, KY, manufactures high-end architectural wood products. He was struggling to keep his furniture and fixture company alive in a construction recession. His sales were soft and his competition was fierce. Then a dream contract appeared—a contractor for Disney World asked Cowart to supply cabinets and other wood products for a housing development. The job had to be completed within 95 days, and Cowart and Co., with only 20 employees, was too small to handle the job so quickly. Cowart decided to take a chance on implementing an idea he discovered that was popular in Europe: join forces with the competition!

He says that he was brought up to believe that the competition was the enemy. Yet here was a dream project, especially in light of the economic situation at the time. Andy developed an alliance with three of his competitors. They divided design, manufacturing, and assembling duties, and completed the $2.5 million contract. This model, *Flexible Manufacturing Networks*, is popular among small- to medium-size firms in western Europe. The philosophy was once accepted and implemented in America among nineteenth century farmers, but has lost favor over the years. The California wine industry employs an adaption—the sharing of some high-cost equipment among boutique wineries. Cowart's experiment was such a success that it has evolved into the Kentucky Wood Manufacturers Network Inc., a nonprofit group with 17 members.

In my community, just a couple of doors down from the Taco Bell, American, Delta, and United Airlines all share a store-front ticket office. Together, they do a great job of serving the local community's needs. There they stand, ten feet apart, American, Delta, and United ticket agents. And, they all get along just fine and so can you! If you have a small business, ask yourself, "What other local business could I share space with?" As we have pointed out, it has become commonplace to find bank braches in large supermarkets—what innovation is available for you? You and a strategic alliance partner, together, could pull more customers than either of you could alone.

I recently delivered a presentation at Business Technology Association's annual meeting. Traditionally, these had been dealers offering sales and service in photocopiers and other office machines. With the explosion of computers in the workplace over the past decade or so, they found themselves up against the value-added resellers (VARs) who sell and service computer equipment. Now many of these traditional office machine dealers have developed strategic alliances with VARs to completely handle the machine and computer equipment needs of their customers.

Another interesting twist on competitors developing strategic alliances can be found in Denver, CO. It's called the Denver Alliance 1000. The Marriott City Center (600 rooms) and the Hyatt Hotels (500 rooms) were both too small to house large conventions needing one hotel with a thousand rooms. The general managers and the city realized they were losing convention business to other cities so they decided to work together. Together they produced a brochure, advertised in meeting industry magazines, held joint site inspections, and joint pre-convention meetings. Through the alliance efforts, the city has averaged three to four additional large conventions a year. Recently, the 1000-plus room Adam's Mark, opened yet the alliance still works.

> *"I have been up against tough competition all my life. I wouldn't know how to get along without it."*
> —Walt Disney

Alliances with Competitors to Open New Markets can be quite beneficial to both.

Helen Chavez Hansen, at La Tapatia Tortilleria in Fresno, CA, shared with me her success story of developing a strategic alliance with two other tortilla manufacturers to serve a large regional customer. Neither she nor her competitors could properly service the large food retailer since tortillas in California are delivered fresh. An alliance was created with El Aguillea in Salinas (in Central California) and with Tia Rosa in Sacramento (in Northern California). They formulated the tortillas to the exact specifications of the private brand they had created and delivered fresh to the individual stores. The added benefit that the alliance partners received was also selling their own brand of tortillas to the stores, getting double the benefit from the alliance relationship.

On a much larger scale, imagine officials from bitter rivals in computer manufacturing amiably swapping sales ideas. Seem unlikely? Nevertheless, there they were—executives from America's elite high-tech companies—Compaq, Dell Computers, Microsoft Corp., and Sun Microsystems, gathered in a nondescript conference room in Tokyo's Kojimachi business district in Japan. Greeting one another like old friends, laughing and swapping jokes before sitting down to lunch to explore ideas about tackling markets and expanding sales in this toughest of markets. This was a first in 1993. Intriguing isn't it, what can make such strange bedfellows? The computer industry executives believed that age old adage, "United we stand; divided we fall." The adage had a particularly potent meaning in their struggle to crack what is often perceived as the impenetrable Japanese market.

Strategic Alliances for Buying Parity go by names such as buying cooperatives or buying groups.

An example is the American Dental Cooperative (ADC) in St. Louis, MO. Started in the mid-1970s, this cooperative is owned by less than two dozen members. They are North American dental supply distributors that sell to dentists' offices.

The ADC members came together in an alliance for buying parity to "level the playing field" as they called it. Buying as a group, they can get prices similar to that of the two giants in their industry. The cooperative has even created their own private label, Quala brand, to compete with other manufacturer plain wrap brands. The Quala label gives them additional sales and ability to compete at reduced price points. This type of "strength-in-numbers" buying alliance can easily be found in many industries, maybe even yours.

Similar to this buying parity alliance, is the Number One Network in Effingham, IL. About the same age as ADC, Number One members service the printing industry. It supplies consumables, (both name brand and under their own private label) and equipment to printers across North America.

A list of Buying Group Benefits from *Office Dealer* Magazine:

Lower product costs

Lower operating costs

Industry information

Education and training

Networking

Pricing guidelines

Competitive information

Advertising support

Catalogs

Credit information

Reduced-price services

Alliances with Competitors to Build an Industry in a specific geographical location can serve a number of competitors.

In Southern Ontario, Canada, a group of craft (specialty) breweries formed a cooperative alliance to raise the awareness of craft brewing in the area. The six breweries, ranging in size from two employees to 200 employees, all competitors, got together to create the *Ale Trail*. The idea would bring visitors to the area, increase awareness in craft brewing, and increase sales.

The six brewers also received financial grants from Canadian agencies, both federal and provincial, to make a greater impact possible. They hired Mary Cocivera of Cocivera Communications in Ontario to be the *Ale Trail* coordinator. They created seven "Open House Sundays" between April and October for visitations to the breweries and punctuated the events with *Ale Trail* maps, coasters, T-shirts, posters, restaurant table tents, a website (www.*AleTrail*.on.ca), and passports. Guests could visit all six breweries on the trail, get their passports stamped and receive an *Ale Trail* poster free. The overall attendance in the first year (1998) was 10,000 person-visits.

The Recreation Vehicle (RV) industry has had its share of problems. Manufacturers and dealers had become adversaries and, to make matters worse, the public's perception of RVs was that of trailers on wheels. And who bought them—trailer trash. The reality was the opposite: RVs have become so advanced in design and amenities that they now sell for big dollars.

The Recreation Vehicle Industry Association (manufacturers) and Recreation Vehicle Dealers Association got together and launched a program called "Go RVing." It is a multimillion-dollar print and broadcast campaign predominantly funded by an assessment on all new units built. The goal is to change the perception of their target consumers (baby boomers) to what RV life really could be. In the first two years of the campaign, the public's awareness climbed to 22% from the previous 9%.

Strategic Alliances to Beat Competition

An example, Coca-Cola, finally acknowledged the very effective strategies of its main competitor, Pepsi, and decided to make some improvements in distribution through alliance relationships. "It isn't that there are any problems with Coke's numbers," claims a *Wall Street Journal* article. "On the contrary, the company has emerged from its strongest decade ever. Coke's profit growth and stock price have been robust. Through an aggressive push abroad, it now gets fully 80% of its profits from overseas. And in the U.S., it has maintained a solid market share lead over Pepsi—41% to 33%—while deftly swiping Pepsi's major restaurant customers." But the decline in carbonated soft drink consumption seems imminent and Coke has developed an alliance with Nestlé.

The new company, a joint venture, Coca-Cola Nestlé Refreshments Company, is based in Tampa, FL. From Coke came experts in bottling, personnel, and law. From Nestlé came experts in marketing, technical research, and finance. Their goal—to be very profitable by the end of the decade and the world leader in their product category. Coke-Nestlé was born when Coke, the world's biggest soft drink company, and Nestlé, the world's biggest food company formed to make canned and bottled coffees and teas for a worldwide market. Nestlé, putting its coffee-making technology together with Coke's worldwide distribution system, launched its first coffee drink in Seoul, South Korea as far back as October 1991.

Another example of developing an alliance to beat competition is the Sun/IBM alliance to compete with Microsoft. Sun Microsystems and International Business Machines both manufacture computers and are fierce competitors. In 1998, Microsoft had about an 80% market share of the computer operating systems sold. Sun's Java operating system, a fledgling with promise, caught IBM's attention. The relationship benefits both in offering the market an alternative to Microsoft's Windows system in certain applications. This is one of several ways to keep the giant in check.

Alliances to Block New Competitors

Two California telephone companies, GTE and Pacific Bell, entered into an alliance agreement. The agreement blocked Metropolitan Fiber Systems (MFS), a Competitive Access Provider (CAPS), from developing a fiber optics dual communications system to insure the University of California at Los Angeles (UCLA) service in case of an emergency. Paul Childers, network planning section manager at GTE, told me the CAPS sole objective is finding ways to undercut pricing to local phone companies' major business clients.

Childers explained that local telephone companies are regulated but the CAPS are not—this creates a major challenge for local telephone companies in maintaining their business customers, but it allows residents to enjoy a lower service cost than they would without the large business customers. In an effort to maintain local business accounts, competitors GTE and Pacific Bell partnered for a common goal. Pacific Bell allowed GTE to lay cable within Pac Bell's boundaries so both could deliver on UCLA's request and they successfully beat their collective unregulated competitor. This multimillion dollar contract was signed by UCLA, GTE, and Pacific Bell in September 1993 at a gala ceremony—cementing the utilities' hold on another of their profitable business accounts.

Strategic Alliances for Product Development

Chrysler and Westinghouse collaborated to develop a practical electric vehicle. A recent multimillion dollar joint project was intended to develop an advanced electric motor and power controller that would boost acceleration and operating range between charges in Chrysler electric vehicles—two previous key limitations. Either of these large enterprises would have been hard-pressed to do this on their own.

Strategic Alliances for Research

The Environmental Protection Agency (EPA)/Amoco (oil company) tests found costly rules that were focused on the wrong part of plants. The study known as the Yorktown Project employed an alliance between unlikely partners. It started out as a chance meeting of old acquaintances aboard a Chicago-to-Washington flight. One was an EPA employee and the other was an Amoco employee. It was plenty of work, and came close to doom, but the relationship prevailed. The result was that the EPA had a hands-on opportunity to research, and found that many of their assumptions were incorrect; Amoco was relieved of costs and delays resulting from the improperly focused rules.

Another alliance between GM and the federal government has taken a lesson and created a collaborative effort adapted from Japan's elaborate ties between its government and key industries. The consortia have been working on electric car technology. During a first-ever gathering of more than 200 federal scientists from 12 leading national research laboratories with GM's own engineers and scientists, they said they expect to deny foreign auto makers access to the fruits of their joint research.

Strategic Alliances for Manufacturing and Construction

The construction industry has been forced to partner because of the litigation explosion over the past couple of decades. What the industry currently calls "partnering" is having all the key people involved on a project attend a workshop. There are four basic components to a construction project: the owner, the general contractor, architectural and engineering, and the sub-contractors—all are required to attend a workshop lasting from one to five days. They air grievances about each other and iron out differences. Doing this allows them to write a partnering charter, which all in attendance sign. Basically, they agree to complete a project on time, within budget, and without litigation. The idea started at the Army Corps of Engineers and has spread to other government and private sectors.

The Arizona Department of Transportation has made partnering an integral part of its process. For example, a $52 million bid project yielded an average time saved of 19.45%, a savings of $418,203 for Arizona DOT, and a total project savings for all involved of $2,329,026. This is just one example of the many projects where partnering has saved both time and money.

Strategic Alliances Between Private Business and State-Owned Foreign Businesses can be risky and, they can be profitable.

In 1995, Honeywell Inc. and the China National Petrochemical Corporation (Sinopec) formalized an existing relationship (a cooperative joint venture). In a five-year agreement, Honeywell will help Sinopec achieve its goal of becoming a world-class refining and petrochemical corporation by the year 2000.

Honeywell believes their technology solutions provide enhanced control of processing operations, which will improve Sinopec's production capability, tangibly improve energy efficiency, reduce emissions, and support the environment. What Honeywell gets out of the alliance is double the sales to Sinopec's 38 enterprises. Honeywell anticipates a minimum of $75 million in new sales over the five years.

Strategic Alliances for Distribution like the one developed by Coca-Cola and Nestlé Foods for distributing Nestlé iced coffee drink in Korea.

This relationship delivered benefits to both parties. Coke had the channel of distribution and Nestlé had a product that didn't directly compete with their existing products. Maximizing the marketing value you receive from any partner is crucial for alliances to survive.

Non-exclusive agreements also serve. Steelcase, Inc., the world's largest manufacturer of office furniture and office environments, distributes its products through an independent dealer network. These dealers have the ability to sell other lines and offer accessory products from other manufacturers to complete their own product line and to better fulfill the needs of their customers. Steelcase will not sell directly, only through its dealers.

Independent contractors find that some companies—like State Farm Insurance Companies—demand exclusivity. In contrast, the sports and clothing industries work well with multiple-line representatives. State Farm's alliance with their agents is called the Marketing Partnership. Under this umbrella, the elements of the alliance (contract, compensation, renewal ownership, co-op advertising, and termination) can be found. State Farm gives their agents everything they need to conduct business, and it also sells them other items to make improvements. Part of this partnership is computer hardware and software available for lease, and, because it continually upgrades the system, State Farm shoulders the capital investment costs.

Strategic Alliances with Your Customers can be very rewarding.

A few years ago, I received an excited telephone call from Robert Rickenbach, president and founder of Rifocs Corp., a manufacturer of fiber optics and metering devices in Camarillo, CA. He had just returned from a meeting in Denver where he accepted, for Rifocs, the Small Supplier of the Year Award from Lockheed Martin's Astronautics Group. I was moved when he told me that he had used the transparencies from my presentation to his sales representatives in his presentation to Lockheed Martin, and owed part of his success to the ideas from my previous book, *The Art of Partnering*.

He told me the relationship with Lockheed Martin was cemented the first day that a Lockheed Martin employee arrived at his business. The employee arrived from San Diego (a four-hour drive) and discovered that he had brought the wrong software. He told Robert that they would just have to get started the next week when he could bring the correct software. Robert asked if it was software that could be purchased off the shelf at a local retailer. The employee said it could be found easily but the money was not in the budget. Robert told him to go buy it that day so they could get the project started without delay and Rifocs would cover the cost overrun. This is how a quality relationship gets started.

Vendor Managed Inventory (VMI)

Coupled with the idea of VMI, you will find Electronic Data Interchange (EDI), Just-In-Time deliveries (JIT) and Integrated Supply (I/S), another term for sole sourcing. While there are several good books on these ideas, it is important to review the W.I.I.F.Y. (what's in it for you), these ideas deliver. As distribution moves closer to Supply Chain Integration, the resulting benefits for those who participate are many. Your benefits include:

Improved inventory control

Reduced vendor base

Increased product and/or supply turns

Reduced inventory investment

Reduction of transaction costs

Improved service levels

Increased sales

Reduction in out-of-stocks

Improved profit margins

Reduction of purchasing staff

Strategic Alliances with Your Suppliers can mean the difference between failure and success.

This is unfortunate for suppliers that did not develop strategic alliances with their customers, because they are finding it tough going. Big firms are slashing their vendor rolls and working more closely with a select few. Xerox has reduced their suppliers from 5,000 to 500, Motorola from 10,000 to 3,000, and Digital Equipment from 9,000 to 3,000. A lot of suppliers were left out in the cold.

As American companies shrink the number of suppliers, they are putting more energy into the remaining relationships, and are even willing to pay a premium on the theory that getting things right initially is cheaper in the long run. This is in contrast to how we think of American business for the last 60 years or so, functioning within the paradigm of adversary relationships. Squeezing the lifeblood from your supplier had become standard.

Fresh out of school in the mid-1970s, and as a supplier to retailers, I was warned frequently about large companies having a strategy of literally taking over their suppliers' business. This was done by offering orders at an increasing pace that would require additional capital investment on the part of the supplier. Then, when the supplier was deep in debt, the big customer would slow down or stop ordering. The supplier would then be in deep financial trouble and the customer would buy a controlling share and own the supplier. This method of taking over a supplier was often credited to Sears (because that's who was the most famous for doing it) but, in fact, it was the practice of many larger companies. Things have changed. Sears has become a much better partner with its suppliers but others still follow an approach like this.

Another challenge if you have buyers in your company, is to be certain that they support your relationship. Too often buyers come in and squeeze suppliers to appear to you their employer as a hero. Even worse is a dishonest buyer. There was a *Wall Street Journal* article that detailed a situation where a J.C. Penney buyer was sentenced to 18 months in prison and fined $50,000 for accepting $1 million in bribes and kickbacks from vendors and sales representatives. This is not exactly the way to build lasting relationships.

One of my panel members at a three-day program I delivered, Brian Potter, VP, 3M Home and Commercial Care Division, told his customers at the 1997 Building Service Contractors Association International's CEO retreat in Los Cabos, Mexico, that his goal was to become their partner in developing the new products that they might need to better serve their customers. Also, he wanted to help them obtain new business by working the relationships that other 3M divisions might already have with their prospects. Brian was simply looking for partners who *wanted* to partner with him. Which of your suppliers truly want to develop alliances with you? Spend your time building those relationships that will help you to serve your market and improve your bottom line. When you commit to a closer relationship with your suppliers, it helps them and they can offer you a better total value package. Not always the best price, but the best total value.

Another way to build a strong alliance with your supplier is to ask them, "What can I do for you?" I recently delivered a seminar titled *Dealing with Vendors* to the National School Supply and Equipment Association. Wanting to do something a little different, I interviewed several of the industry manufacturers and asked them, "What can your customers do for you?" The initial responses were interesting in that they told me what they did for their customers. Why? Because that is their usual business paradigm. Wanting to turn the selling paradigm around, I kept pushing. Eventually, I discovered several issues the manufacturers had with how the school supply and equipment end-users would buy. Working with the manufacturers, we came up with about ten strategies for the end-users to buy better from the manufacturers in a way that served the manufacturers. In turn, we offered additional "value" to the end-users for changing their buying habits. You can take this idea in both directions: what can you do for your suppliers, and what your customers can do for you. Amazing how we can serve one another if we just put a little energy into it!

The Fuji Factor

Recently, I presented an opening keynote for an association of graphic arts suppliers. During preprogram research, I interviewed a supplier to the industry, Stan Freimuth, president at Fuji Photo Film U.S.A, Industrial Imaging Group, Itasca, IL. Through additional interviews, it became obvious to me that among the major suppliers to the industry, Fuji was by far the most advanced in building quality relationships with its dealers.

The Fuji factor is a model that more manufacturers should embrace and more purchasers should demand of their suppliers. Wouldn't you rather have a supplier relationship that could grow and improve over time? This is only possible with the right kind of supplier. Steelcase, in Grand Rapids, MI, is another great example of a quality supplier with a policy designed to protect its dealer network. As we mentioned earlier, if a customer tries to go around the dealer and buy direct from Steelcase, Steelcase will simply give up the business rather than leave its dealers out. That's integrity!

The key elements to Fuji's success are as follows:

- A limited number of dealers offering their products to their market
- Manufactured products of the highest quality with zero defects as the norm
- Build tight relationships with a limited dealer network
- Seek constructive feedback from dealers and act upon the ideas shared
- Consistency of leadership—Stan has been the president since 1983 when Fuji opened shop in the United States. Other companies in its industry have had numerous changes in leadership during that same time period
- Accessibility—several dealers told me they could pick up the telephone and easily reach Stan
- Trust—when I asked Stan about building quality relationships with his dealers, he said, "It doesn't come easy, it's hard work."

Alliances on the Internet

The Internet has changed the way many industries do business.

A perfect example of an Internet strategic alliance is Lifelines (www.lifelines.com). Kailash Narayan created a site that is an alliance between his company and several health and employee productivity related companies. The site lets corporate decision makers know what is available to them in the area of employee effectiveness and productivity. The information on the site helps people to improve their effectiveness through improved health and, eventually, optimal wellness. Check the site out. It's worth a few minutes of your time.

Your current business may be a result of the Internet explosion and you might be looking for an alliance partner because of your business growth. The Internet holds many pitfalls and, yet, many possibilities. Don't shy away from Internet commerce; just don't get wrapped up in the emotion of riches and make bad choices.

Follow the principles stated throughout this book, ask the questions, do your homework—just because it is the Internet, it doesn't mean it is magic in itself. You need to add to your Internet activity whatever makes your business unique.

Mastermind Alliances, also known as strategic alliances for individual development, can assist you in eclipsing your competition.

This holds true for both your career and your enterprise. I belong to a geographical mastermind alliance, called Gold Coast Speakers, which consists of other professional speakers and consultants. We started meeting early in 1989 and have continued to get together about once a month or so. This is a confidential environment where each can share their gifts and also receive counsel on important business, career, and personal issues. I do not believe I would have survived in my speaking career without this relationship. The members of my mastermind alliance are some very special and giving people. The group consists of not more than a dozen members that are geographically close. This allows us to get together regularly. We rotate from home to home, each member having the opportunity to host meetings. We make it simple for the host by having pizza delivered.

Another mastermind alliance success story is the Palm Springs Breakfast Club. A couple of years ago, I interviewed Tim Ellis, general manager at the Riveria Resort & Racquet Club in Palm Springs, CA, for an article about Palm Springs' strategic alliance with other California cities to draw tourists to the state. He told me about his downtown Palm Springs mastermind alliance which consisted of general managers from seven other deluxe hotels, the convention center director, and the owner of the aerial tram. They meet every Wednesday and rotate member locations weekly. They discuss issues uniquely important to the hospitality business in downtown Palm Springs.

I recently spoke with Tim. He is no longer at the Riveria. He started his own company, Lathom Hotels. He bought one hotel and leased another. Both hotels feature suites with full kitchens. He started his company to serve a neglected niche in town, long-term retired guests. He told me that much of his success comes from the networking relationships in the Palm Springs Breakfast Club. He said that he could not have picked up and done the same thing in another town. And yes, he still belongs to the alliance.

> *"In this unbelievable universe in which we live, there are no absolutes. Even parallel lines, reaching into infinity, meet somewhere yonder."*
> —Pearl S. Buck, 1962

> *"I can never stand still. I must explore and experiment. I am never satisfied with my work. I resent the limitations of my own imagination.*
> —Walt Disney

Chapter 3

★★★★★★

How to Find & Select Alliance Partners

★★★★★★

"Without wearing any mask we are conscious of, we have a special face for each friend."

—Oliver Wendell Holmes, Sr.

★★★★★★

"Grief can take care of itself, but to get the full value of joy you must have somebody to divide it with."

—Mark Twain

Finding an Alliance Partner

✔ *Partnering Axiom Number One: You can only partner with someone or an organization that wants to partner.*

Time after time, people come up to me after a seminar and ask, "How do I partner with somebody who doesn't want to partner?" My answer is always the same, "You don't!" As you start your search, keep this in mind.

Where Does One Find Great Alliance Partners? Your perfect alliance partner could be around the corner, down the street, or across the country. You just never know. There are several places to start (but please, do not make the mistake of checking one area, coming up empty-handed, and quitting.) Start now in each of the following areas. Just one contact in each area per week is a reasonable start.

• **Your suppliers** are a good place to start in your search for the perfect mate. They know your competitors and other local business people from a different perspective than you. You can learn about their buying habits, bill-paying habits, and other important information about them. Start talking to your suppliers. They are generally a wealth of knowledge.

Make a list of the suppliers you will contact this week:

_____

_____

_____

• **Your customers** are another great place to look. They have most likely done some business with the person or company that you are seeking. They, too have a unique window through which they have viewed your potential alliance partner. Make a list of customers whose opinions you value:

_____

_____

_____

- **Your professional or trade association** is a great place to search if you want to build an alliance with either competitors or suppliers. The executive director of the association is usually the person who is most in tune with the players in your industry. Call this person and ask for a list of possible alliance partners:

_____

_____

_____

- **Newspapers and trade magazines** offer current information on the movers and shakers in many industries. They compare, research and generally dig up interesting bits of information about businesses and key players. Study these publications as a source for selecting possible alliance partners.

Make a list now of the publications in which you will search:

_____

_____

_____

- **Local successful business people** can be found at the chamber of commerce activities and mixers, civic service clubs, charitable organizations, and even local seminars.

Make a list of local organizations you will visit. Also list local people you respect and will call this month:

_____

_____

_____

- **Study groups and mastermind alliances.** If you can't find one, start one with people in your community.

_____

_____

_____

- **Think about outside professionals** including, consultants, lawyers, and accountants.

  _____

  _____

  _____

- Lastly, give yourself some time to look around on the **Internet**.

  _____

  _____

  _____

Selecting an Alliance Partner

Identifying a Strategic Alliance Partner's Core Values is a good start when you begin your search for an alliance partner. If you and your alliance partner's core values do not align well, you are heading for a train wreck. In contrast, when your values align easily, synergies become possible, and maybe even easy. First, compare your core values with the five values I have listed below. Be clear on what both you, and your company, are all about. Then, as you start looking at possible partners, seek to understand their values and try to determine if your circles of interest overlap. The more your circles of interest overlap, the better the chance for your future alliance to be successful and lasting.

If you have little information on your potential partner (but believe them to be a good choice), first try working with them on a small project. Though the project is small, be sure it is somewhat difficult (at least complex enough to stress you both a bit). Then wait and watch to see how they operate under pressure. You will then have a better idea about their viability as an alliance partner.

> _"If you know the enemy and you know yourself, you need not fear the result of a hundred battles. If you know yourself but not the enemy, for every victory gained you will also suffer a defeat. If you know neither the enemy nor yourself, you will succumb in every battle."_
>
> —Sun Tzu, _The Art of War_, (c. 500 B.C.)

I have been sharing this quotation with my seminar attendees for years. I suggest we change the words, "the enemy" to "your alliance partner." Now go back and read the quotation again. It's quite powerful! Understand your needs, strengths, *and* weaknesses. Be sure to also understand those of your alliance partners. Do this, and your success is nearly certain. Trust yourself and your partner to make the right decisions.

Trust

Recently, I presented a Partnering program in Calgary, Alberta. I met two very interesting men with whom I shared the podium, Jamie Clarke and Alan Hobson. Both from Calgary, they had a dream of ascending to the peak of Mt. Everest. They had tried twice, but their dream eluded them. Finally, on their third attempt they were successful—they had triumphed. In their book, *The Power of Passion, Achieve Your Own Everests* (written prior to their third attempt), I found a commanding passage that caught my attention:

> *"Once trust is lost in any relationship, it is like a mirror struck by a stone. Although all the tiny pieces can be glued back into position, the mirror always shows the cracks."*
>
> —Alan Hobson & Jamie Clarke

If someone takes advantage of you, betrays a trust, lies, cheats, steals, or generally rakes you over the coals—from that time on you know it could happen again. Actually, you are not thinking it could happen again—in the back of your mind, you are wondering, *WHEN are they going to do it again?* Warren Benis said in his book *Leaders—Strategies for Taking Charge* that "trust is the glue that binds an organization." I'll add, "Or an alliance." For alliance relationships, trust is the necessary element to move the possible alliance from inertia to action. Without **the Trust Factor**, alliance relationships are sure to fail.

Silicon Graphics' CFO, Stan Meresman, stresses that developing trust is critical. He says there's no substitute for spending time to develop a relationship and coming through for your partner. As every alliance is going to have problems, he believes the key is informal communication and finding out what's really going on.

In trusting another, you're continually putting yourself at risk. It's the process of taking necessary risks that allows the building of alliance relationships. At times you are certain to be disappointed, but hopefully these disappointments will be few compared to the availability of beneficial experiences. Some of the *soft* benefits both organizations will receive are: open communication, mutual respect, appreciation, commitment, security, pride, and confidence. To help you in building trust and creating an environment where all partners have the ability to grow fully comfortable with one another, I suggest you:

1. Recognize and reinforce the relationship behaviors you want of your alliance partners.

2. Break down the communication barriers between your and your alliance partner's organizations.

3. Quarterly, or at least semi-annually, complete a **Relationship Value Update** form (found in Chapter 6), and then encourage your alliance partner to do the same. Send your completed form to your alliance partner and ask your partner to send theirs to you.

4. Be a role model of the behaviors you believe are important for alliance partners. Remember, if you want to change the world, you must start with yourself.

Trust wisely, and with caution. Do the right things, looking toward the long-term rather than the short term. Help your alliance partner to help you. Let the trust build and grow over the years. Do these things, and the benefits that you and your partner share will multiply.

Tolerance

Unfortunately, the word tolerance has become a cliché that too easily rolls off the tongue. This is true in both the political and business arenas. For an alliance to work, the core value of tolerance must be *cherished and practiced* by all the alliance members. When you can accept the value of an idea rather than be concerned about whose inspiration it was, you will truly exhibit tolerance. When you exhibit tolerance, the by-product of your effort is understanding. When you understand your alliance partner and their needs, you will work toward creating value for them in their areas of need.

One of the important values derived from a strategic alliance is innovation. Too often, especially when a small organization partners with a large one, protectionism comes into play. In large organizations, the partnering pitfall of a *not-invented-here* mentality can stifle growth and synergy. This is most often noticed when there is a lack of commitment toward the alliance from the senior management. Through increased tolerance for the ideas of others, innovation, synergy, and growth becomes possible.

> *"Laws alone cannot secure freedom of expression;*
> *in order that every man present his views without*
> *penalty there must be a spirit of tolerance in the*
> *entire population."*
> —Albert Einstein, 1950

Cooperation

In my full-day seminars, I generally lead an exercise where several members of the audience stand in a circle, facing the center. Once blindfolded, I give them each the rope to hold that is tied together at the ends. I instruct the group to make a square. This exercise was created to show how much is possible when the participants cooperate and work together rather than separately.

Success is only possible through an attitude of cooperation. During the rope exercise, it is always interesting who shows up as the leader. The leader directs the group in successfully completing the square. The leader is rarely the organization's boss. Growth is the natural outcropping of cooperation.

Abraham Lincoln once said, "A drop of honey catches more flies than a gallon of gall." While I sometimes have a challenge in this area in my own life, I know Abe was right. Today, most businesses want to grow and that is an important reason for developing strategic alliances. Remember, kindness leads to cooperation and cooperation creates an environment for growth. There are always prices to pay, and kindness is one of those prices. Pay it gladly!

> *"Where two people are writing the same book,*
> *each believes he gets all the worries and only half*
> *the royalties."*
> —Agatha Christe, 1955

Commitment

Caring enough about your strategic alliance and its members is the necessary foundation to making a commitment. It is also what will help to smooth out the potholes on the way. It is this element that allows each partner in an alliance to feel he will be heard, and will be reasonably safe from criticism. Additionally, there is also the commitment that is necessary to the function of leadership, and at times, the ability to follow when another is currently leading.

The way to develop commitment is to understand emotional ownership. Emotional Ownership is the fire in the belly that is evident among some people. There are an art and science to developing your emotional ownership. The science is learning the path and where you are on it. The art is how you experience the path. More on this idea in Chapter 6.

"The beauty of a strong, lasting commitment is often best understood by a man incapable of it."
—Murray Kempton, 1955

Mutuality

A strategic alliance must be an institution where individuals, organizations, and companies come together to develop a relationship of trust, tolerance, cooperation, commitment, and mutuality. The result is similar to a successful marriage. Strategic alliances have much in common with the institution of marriage. In both, the benefits of belonging must outnumber the possibilities available singularly, without the relationships.

These values are prevalent in every successful strategic alliance I have studied. In a symbiotic relationship of two dissimilar organisms in close association or union, especially where this is advantageous to both, each finds a way to co-exist. The alliance partner you select must exhibit these core values, or your alliance is doomed from its inception.

Couple the above with *the desire to win* and you now have the foundation for successful strategic alliances. These alliances form the framework for a supercharged marketing campaign and business strategy based on a mutually equitable relationship. I suggest this is because strategic alliances are only as strong as their weakest member. When the weakest member does not have the desire to win, they become nothing more than a remora. That's a fish that adheres to another and enjoys a free ride, hanging on and benefiting from another's efforts and contributing nothing! They can only be dislodged with great difficulty and pain. Mutuality is the *must have* ingredient in a successful partnering alliance.

> *"That which is mutually equitable is lasting."*
> —Glenn Bostrom, Founder,
> Bostrom Association Management Corp., 1965

> *"Keep your eyes wide open before marriage, half shut afterwards."*
> —Benjamin Franklin, *Poor Richard's Almanac*, 1738

The 10 Critical Qualities to Look In An Alliance Partner

1. Your partner wants to win. Pick a partner who is already a winner. There is no good reason to partner with anyone else. The relationship with a weak partner will only bring you or your organization down. Both you and your partner must have a desire to win—to want to do better—to be useful in creating only what will be valuable to all concerned.

2. Your partner must understand that they are ultimately responsible for their own success. A person who will partner because he or she understands the value of synergies is a great partner. Important, too, is knowing when partnering is and is not the best choice for a situation. *Caveat Pars* (Beware of Partner)! Accountability is a double-edged sword. Don't always assume that your partner is looking out for your best interest. You both are human—and as such, are susceptible to the fault of not always acting in *your* partner's best interest.

3. Your partner must be an active listener. To truly keep in touch with the heartbeat of an alliance, active listening is a critical skill. This helps you to know what you need to do and when the other side is falling behind in their commitment to you. Alertness from both sides equals mutual success.

4. Your partner must understand and care about what drives your business. Because successful partnering is about synergies, you must consistently give and receive additional value in the relationship. The only way to add value is to know what it is that creates value for your partner. This is only possible with an understanding of the needs and goals of your partner.

5. Your partner must respond to, and act on, feedback. The only possibility for a forward and beneficial movement in any organization is with leaders who are willing to accept council. Not one of us is smart enough to know it all!

6. Your partner must be flexible, especially when events or circumstances are not what were expected. If you don't have the ability to change direction when the road ahead is washed out, you'll most likely find yourself wishing for rescuers as you float uncontrollably down the stream. Flexibility is absolutely necessary because things will never be exactly as we expect. Silicon Graphics' Stan Meresman believes in "staying flexible enough to evolve our relationships."

7. Your partner must be trusting, trustworthy, and with integrity, respecting all with whom they come in contact. During my research, I interviewed employees at Steelcase and found this to be the common thread uniting all the employees from the factory floor to the executive suite. You can't always be looking over your shoulder in an alliance relationship. Partnering with people who are trusting and trustworthy relieves a major nuisance, one that you can do without.

8. Your partner seeks win/win arrangements and solutions. It is true that you must look after yourself. But if that's all you do, you're of little value as a partner. You must win for the sake of your organization. And your partner must do the same. You do not want a partner who sees the world as a zero-sum game. You want a partner that is interested in making the pie bigger, so everybody gets more. This creates a desire for both of you to continue in the relationship. The partnering advantage becomes stronger the longer the relationship lasts.

9. Your partner must understand that partnering is a relationship of interdependence. Not dependently or independently, but together, you are weaving a tapestry. Visualize your partner and yourself as overlapping circles. The parts that overlap are your area of mutual interest and value. The greater the overlap, the greater the mutual interest and value. This overlapping area is your area of interdependence. Working together for mutual improvement is one of the great benefits received from partnering.

10. You and your partner must have great chemistry. If both people or organizations exude many of the above qualities, and have good chemistry, it is an unstoppable alliance. This is what we all desire to achieve.

Credentials of Your Future Alliance Partner

- The ability to do and produce what your partner perceives you can (individual or company) through skills, technology, and relationships. Alliance agreements are of little value when a partner cannot deliver what is promised. If I have hotdog buns and my partner cannot deliver the promised frankfurters, who needs that partner?

- Have something new to bring to the party. If you're selling hamburgers, then lettuce, pickles, and catsup are necessary but not innovative. Building an alliance with someone who only has these to offer is fine, but limiting. Suppose someone could supply you with all of the above, *and* had guacamole? The guacamole is different, thereby allowing you to create a new product—the guacamole burger (it is a silly example, but it makes the point). A partner that had an innovative method to produce fat-free fried chicken would also be bringing something new to the party, allowing you to increase your penetration within a limited local market.

- Having the financial ability to stay-the-course. If your alliance partner has the means to continually contribute their agreed share, your continued success is promising.

- Cultural compatibility, operates from integrity, and is willing to challenge existing corporate paradigms.

- Complimentary core strengths, allowing for benchmarking of overlapping capabilities and the elimination of "recreating of the wheel syndrome."

- The ability to think not only strategically, but also tactically.

Following are three relationship realities, unpleasant as they are. These realities will have a powerful effect, good or bad, on the success of your alliance relationship.

- People do not change after marriage!

- What you see is what you get!

- You deserve the partner you select!

I'm sure you know someone who thought they would *change* their spouse after their marriage. Did your friend's spouse change? Of course not! Your friend made their bed and now they get to lie in it. The same will apply to your strategic alliance partner. Who they are is important.

I recommend visiting your potential partner at their place of business. This may seem a bit on the edge, but . . . Set up an appointment to visit for say, Tuesday, but show up on Monday. When they say you're a day early, say, "I'm sorry, my mistake. Can we visit anyway?"

If they are less than willing to let you look around, I'd be suspicious and consider the situation a red flag. Why is this? On a personal level, when you have a party at your house, don't you always clean up, get special food for the party and so on? Sure you do. You want to put on your *best* face and it is not really who you are every day. It is not how you live. You want to catch your potential alliance partner in their *real life*, not with the special face they put on for you. Knowing who your partner really is eliminates much of the need for conflict resolution and exit agreements.

If you are clear about what you have to offer an alliance partner and what you want from an alliance, you have discovered *purpose*. When you have a purpose in developing a strategic alliance, your plan seems to arrive on its own. The hows and whys are not always clear, but what does become clear is how to devise a road map for success. Burn these words, half a millennium old, into your mind as you start your search for an alliance partner:

"Obstacles cannot crush me.
Every obstacle yields to stern resolve.
He who is fixed to a star does not change his mind."

—Leonardo da Vinci (c. 1500)

Chapter 4

★★★★★★

Steps in Developing Your Alliance

★★★★★★

"What sets us against one another is not our aims—they all come to the same thing—but our methods, which are the fruit of our varied reasoning."

—Saint-Exupéry, 1939

Introduction of a New Paradigm

Partnering, to be successful, must start at the top of any organization. Leaders determine the culture. Leaders set the policy. Leaders (good leaders) reward the behaviors they want repeated. If the leaders have an Emotional Ownership in the partnering, so will the rest of the organization.

The introduction of a new paradigm (the Partnering Paradigm) to your organization need not be difficult if approached with reason. Prove it to yourself with this simple test: draw yourself a bath of lukewarm water, get in the tub, and relax. Next, open the water valve allowing only hot water into the tub. Let the hot water run for as long as you can stand the heat. Use a thermometer to record the water temperature.

The next day, draw yourself a bath at that same maximum temperature. Chances are you'll jump out of the tub because the water will be too hot for you. Why was it tolerable before? You slowly became accustomed to the change. For many, too much change too quickly can be a disaster! Give yourself and all the people around you time to adjust to the "hot water" or shifting paradigm. Do this and you are off to a great start.

> *"Better one safe way than a hundred*
> *on which you cannot reckon."*
> —Aesop, *Fables*, (6th c. B.C.)

Your commitment of time is an absolute necessity in developing alliance relationships. An unwillingness to allocate time is an assured road block to successful partnering. Just as in any new endeavor, put your alliance plan into play and avoid the urge to change it before the plan has time to work. It's up to you. Be ready for ridicule from non-believers. It's sure to come.

Doing business through an alliance window will open up new possibilities for your management, production, and marketing strategy as well as your business as a whole. You will learn how to work with others for cost reductions while enjoying greater-than-ever exposure to your current market, as well as to other markets. You can succeed and you can do it with others. The basic idea, repeated often, is to make the pie bigger. This helps others, as well as yourself, to enjoy more pie. While the percentage may remain the same, everybody still gets more pie.

Don't Wait for Perfection. If you do wait, it'll be too late. Windows of alliance opportunity open and they close. Once closed, they may never again be available to you. This does not mean that all windows will be closed, but your first and possibly your best choice could easily slip from your grasp. Your competition will do what you simply thought about. This dilemma has been called *paralysis by analysis.* Don't become paralyzed —you can't make any money that way. Don't wait until you can deal with all your challenges neatly, and all at the same time. Take special notice of the section on emotional ownership in Chapter 6.

> *"There is no more miserable human being than one*
> *in whom nothing is habitual but indecision."*
> —William James, *The Principles of Psychology,* 1892

While studying a challenge is usually considered to be a strength, when you study infinitum, your strength becomes your weakness. The result is a lack of action, or just as devastating, being perceived as not having the ability to make a decision. This can be costly to your business or career. Being perceived by your industry as one who cannot decide can be the kiss of death. You might be excluded from new and exciting partnering alliances because others will not think you can be depended upon. The ability to make decisive and timely decisions is at the root of quality leadership.

> *"Nothing is more difficult, and therefore more*
> *precious, than to be able to decide."*
> —Napoleon I, *Maxims* (1804-15)

On the flip side, taking intelligent risk is crucial to alliance partnering. Taking imprudent, irresponsible, and reckless risks is not what I'm talking about. Early in my career, an executive under whom I worked, repeatedly said to me, "Ed, if you're not making mistakes; I don't need you because you're not taking risks and learning. But, if you keep making the same mistakes I don't need you either, because you're not learning." One of the great values you'll receive from partnering is access to the mistakes of others. This greatly reduces your need to take uninformed risks.

> *"To win without risk is to triumph without glory."*
> —Corneille, *The Cid,* 1636

Steps to Building a Strategic Alliance

Step 1: Monitor

- Have a good reason for developing an alliance and know what you want from it.
- Study your business, observe, and identify areas for improvement.
- Take inventory of core strengths that might be valuable to a potential alliance partner.
- Specifically, define what it is that you want and help others to define what they want and help them to achieve it as quickly as possible.
- Study other industries that have embraced partnering along with the individual companies that have been successful with partnering.
- Study what worked and what did not.
- If partnering was not successful, be sure to understand why.

Step 2: Educate

- Learn about those companies you might consider for strategic alliance arrangements.
- Seek arrangements that create a win/win result for all who participate.
- Ask yourself and your management team important strategic questions.
- What are their (your intended partner) strengths and weaknesses?
- What are your strengths and weaknesses?
- What effect would they have on our business?
- What effect would we have on their business?
- Be sure that the company cultures are complementary and that the people who will make the alliance work have the ability to get along.

Step 3: Select

- Recognize this as a critical step as your future efforts will be built on this foundation.
- Select alliance partnering, and with whom to build your alliance, with knowledge, understanding, and commitment.

- Search for the strongest material for your alliance foundation.

- Select organizations with customer-oriented culture.

- The greater the sophistication of a company and its officers, the more likely a company will enter into alliance relationships.

- Embrace long-term thinking. Alliances are rarely quick fixes, but rather a sound long-term business strategy.

- Target companies, large or small, that can aid you in rapidly and efficiently, reaching the goals of research, technology, production, and marketing.

- Consider the focus of the individuals involved. Be certain that the focus of the partnering relationship is strategic to the individual goals.

- Total organizational ownership in the new alliance. Let your team add to your alliance vision rather than just buy into it.

Step 4: Organize

- Now identify, understand, and put together the possibilities for your alliance.

- Work with internal and external personnel, develop not only your alliance structure, but also your road map.

- The success in blending cultures is pivotal to the successes in any partnering alliance. Take great pains to insure this achievement.

- Access is crucial. Emphasize the importance of understanding and access to the staff of each alliance member.

- Create a convenient communication system for all partners, especially decision makers. Plan procedures to keep relationships between key people of partnering companies open and constantly alive.

- Make sure that all levels of both organizations share the alliance attitude.

- Help employees of both companies to have an emotional ownership in the alliance and its success.

- Allow employees to job swap or share with their counterparts at your alliance partner's organization.

- Stress strong information systems and share information constantly. Systems such as electronic data interchange for document savings, inventory control, materials ordering, production, and advertising.

- Agree on net pricing with your partners and delete "income accounts" (accounting practices) that have nothing to do with your business or the real price of your goods and services. Be cautious of behaviors that only make singular departments look successful.

- Look into the future, plan for the long-term relationship, and encourage strategies that will sustain the relationship through to its conclusion.

- Phasing in the alliance relationship could be a preferred strategy, as this method will allow partners to have a *get acquainted* time. This can assist in the identification of milestones or the need to reassess before moving onto a higher level in the relationship.

- Consider participating in a small cooperative project together with your alliance partner and then study both organization's performance.

- Both parties should thoroughly discuss cooperative budgeting, forecasting, and payment terms.

Step 5: Charter, or the Agreement

- First decide whether your agreement will be a handshake, or an actual contract. All alliance's agreements should be put on paper. This makes it easier for everybody to remember their promises and commitments.

- Include the nature, purpose, and name for your strategic alliance or joint venture.

- The charter, or agreement, should spell out conflict resolution.

- Be ready for conflict and it will be resolved timely and amiably.

- Has an agreed-upon set of procedures in place that will help resolve the issues that arise.

- Include representations, warranties, capital contributions, and mutual covenants in your alliance agreement.

- Inevitably, there will be a need for a mechanism to handle things like price increase discussions, inability to ship, and dispute resolutions.

- Develop a clear agreement on what your goals are and make sure they are measurable.

- Have a formal mechanism for alliance members to identify the goals, milestones, and turning points crucial to the success of the relationship.

- Devise some form of evaluation that will measure how well plans have implemented.

    - relationship changes

    - relationship value updates

    - alliance business plan

    - rewards for success

- Given that each party views the alliance agreement as a business opportunity, the agreement should establish the terms and conditions under which the partners will resolve questions of frustrated business opportunity.

- Consider having the agreement include forms of dispute resolution for more formal arrangements, along with exit strategies as partnering safety valves.

- Have the agreement reviewed by a lawyer. Sure, it can be costly, but unresolvable conflict can be even more costly.

For a joint venture which is generally a more formal relationship, here are some additional considerations:

- Distribution of profits and losses among partners is an important issue to be resolved prior to the completion of the agreement.

- Management, control, and voting issues need to be written into the agreement.

- Insurance and cross-indemnification obligations of each partner need to be included.

- Ownership transferability restrictions and allowances must be stated.

- Responsibility for overhead and administrative expenses and record location needs to be determined.

- Control over bank accounts, inspection, and audits are important issues to resolve.

- In the case of default, dissolution, or termination of a venture, how will the remaining assets or liabilities be distributed to the partners?

Check with your professional or trade association. They may, as does Business Technology Association (800) 247-2176 and others, offer alliance agreement templets that have been developed for their members. The legal templates alone could be worth the cost of membership.

Also, you can contact The Corporate Partnering Institute at (800) 948-1700 for legal and agreement assistance. The checklists at the end of this book are from The Corporate Partnering Institute. Nolo Press has a book titled, *The Partnership Book: How to Write a Partnership Agreement* by Clifford & Warner. They also have several other legal partnership books (www.nolo.com). An important point to remember: partnering (strategic alliances) is different from partnership.

Step 6: Post Agreement

- Regularly review your relationship efforts through Relationship Value Updates. (More about this in the next chapter.)

- Periodically sit down with alliance partners and evaluate whether the relationship should be upgraded, maintained, or downgraded. Be clear on how this is to be done in the alliance agreement.

- To continuously improve your business and the quality of the partnering agreement, share information regularly with partners.

- Discuss opportunities for improvement and ways to enhance performance.

- A favorable public image and stature of all strategic alliance members are necessary to keep the alliance valuable to all.

- You are responsible for selecting and maintaining the alliance you entered into. If at the onset it seems too good to be true—it likely is!

- Understand that inherently in the process, alliance partnering has both benefits and pitfalls.

I asked Dwane Baumgardner, Chairman of Donnelly Corporation in Holland, MI what they do to keep flare-ups from getting to the point where an alliance relationship must be severed. He told me they meet with the right people as soon as possible, no matter what level, making sure that all the right people are involved, and talk through the problem. You'll find that, if you get all the right people there to talk through a problem, almost

100% of the time you're able to work it out. Little things rarely stay little; keep little issues from blowing up into alliance killing situations.

You cannot put a price on relationships. Here are three activities that are crucial to continued successful relationships:

1. *Build rapport* with many people in the organization of your strategic alliance partner. This protects you and the alliance from a situation where your contact leaves the organization and you are left in an alliance without any real relationships.

2. *Keep in touch regularly*, not only when the formal value updates are reviewed. Too often relationships between two organizations can take on the flavor of fire fighting when solving a crisis. Rather, work toward regular positive communication.

3. *Make "Relationship Bank" deposits frequently*. It is difficult to walk into your local bank and ask for half a million dollars just because you're a nice person. You cannot make withdrawals before you make deposits. The same is true in alliance relationships. Do extra things for your alliance partner, just because you want to.

> *"When great causes are on the move in the world,*
> *stirring men's souls, drawing them from their*
> *firesides, casting aside comfort, wealth and the*
> *pursuit of happiness in response to impulses at*
> *once awe-striking and irresistible, we learn that we*
> *are spirits, not animals."*
> —Sir Winston Churchill, 1941

Ten Tips to Developing Outrageously Successful Alliance Relationships

1. Behave toward your alliance partner the way you want them to behave toward you.

2. It's more important to be a good alliance partner and get things done, than to obsess on being right.

3. Make relationship bank deposits before you try to make a withdrawal.

4. Regularly share relationship value updates with your alliance partner.

5. Know what your partner needs.

6. Be clear about what you want from your alliance relationship and what you are willing to give to it.

7. Be committed; always show your confidence and passion toward your alliance.

8. Do more for your alliance partner than you promised; exceed their expectations.

9. Resolve conflict immediately.

10. You can't partner with an organization or individual who doesn't want to be a good partner.

Successfully partnering with your competition is like getting in bed with the enemy

In my seminar with a similar name, I take a humorous look at developing strategic alliances with competitors. To add a different twist, I relate the process to that of a marriage. If the *Steps to Partnering* were too dry and academic, you'll get a kick from the following:

1. Your Search for the Perfect Mate

• Ask yourself, what are you seeking?

• Where should you look?

• What are you willing to give to make the alliance valuable for your partner?

• Understand that people do not change after marriage.

• Remember this: marry in haste and you'll repent at leisure.

2. The Getting-Married Jitters

• Why do you want to go it alone?

• Will you be partners for life or will it have an intended ending date? Well, that depends on your ability to maintain a relationship.

• Can you make it work? That's the $64,000 question.

• Will my partner be faithful? Select well, and there's a good chance for success.

- Living together is not the same as marriage. The commitment is not there. It's easy to leave when the challenges come, and be assured, they will come.

3. Where Are We Going to Live?

- Who is going to cover which geographical areas?
- Will we stumble over each other?
- How will our strengths overlap?
- How will our product and/or service offering compliment one another?
- Will we have to develop new shopping habits (buying habits)?
- Can we share information recovery systems? Are they compatible with each other?

4. Who's Going to Do the Chores?

- Talk about our new responsibilities to each other.
- Share our expectations of each other.
- Put what we talked about, and agreed on, in writing.
- Determine how to administer Relationship Value Updates (RVUs).
- Marriage tends to be a mutual-assistance pact.

5. Tying the Knot

- How do we create synergies, and what kind will it be?
- Is our alliance charter or agreement, sound? Does it serve us both?
- Are we each willing to meet the other more than halfway?
- Are we willing to make Relationship Bank deposits in each other's accounts?
- Do we have what it takes to commit to each another?
- Some say marriage is an institution run by the inmates.

6. Under the Sheets

- Can we be successful cohabitants?
- Do we each understand that we are still responsible for our own success?
- How could actions from my partner's behavior affect my business? How could my behavior affect theirs?

- Are we each willing to confer with one another before we act?
- Can we act quickly to resolve issues?
- Never go to sleep angry with each other.

7. When Your Partner Takes All the Covers

- Can we fight the "Denial Syndrome" when things aren't going well?
- How will we handle conflict? Do we let it fester or do we deal with it quickly?
- Do we understand the adage, "What goes around, comes around?"
- Here's where marriage runs the risk of going from bed to worse.

8. A Visit to the Marriage Counselor

- How will we deal with relationship roadblocks like hidden agendas and insecurity?
- Will we need third-party mediation, and who's going to pay for it?
- What conflict resolution processes can we put into place, and who can we get to help us?
- Will reconciliation be possible?

9. Oh No! Divorce?

- What about infidelity? How much loyalty can we expect from one another?
- Are our differences irreconcilable?
- Will I become immobilized through the conflict?
- Can I finally let go of the relationship?
- How will the separation go?
- How will we divide the community property (especially customers)?

10. We Did It, and Look at All the Profits!

- Are we enjoying our mutual success?
- Has the journey been fulfilling?
- What other alliances are now possible because of our success?
- Are we collecting the rewards?
- Have we celebrated our success?

"When a match has equal partners / then I fear not."
—Aeschylus (c. 478 B.C.)

"Marriage is one long conversation, checkered by disputes."
—Robert Louis Stevenson

10 Success Factors in the Making of an Alliance

1. Crucial Driving Forces. There must be strategic reasons for partners to come together. These reasons must be compelling enough to drive the alliance over the long haul. Without these driving forces, the reasons for the alliance may be abandoned.

2. Complementary Needs and Goals. When the needs and goals of alliance partners are complementary and the strengths and weaknesses are dissimilar, the formula for success is in place.

3. Defined Goals and Objectives. It is important to the success of your alliance to have a working road map. Clearly laying out your goals and objectives leads to a workable plan.

4. Operational Integration. Both organizations must be able to work with one another. It is at the operational level of each organization that the goals and objectives of the alliance will be implemented.

5. Growth Potential. Through alliance relationships, your organization has excellent potential for industry leadership and greater market share. Be sure you and your partner have the capabilities to take advantage of the opportunity.

6. Financial Capability. Each partner must have the capability to grow and nurture the alliance through both activity and financial contributions.

7. Intellectual Property Rights. Intellectual property rights derived from alliance relationships should be clearly laid out at the onset of the relationship. The important value for all the partners involved is reducing the need for conflict resolution through the life of the alliance.

8. Reduce Blind Enthusiasm. Especially at the senior management level, keeping an eye on technological and operational capabilities of all involved is crucial. Lack of capabilities can easily be overlooked early in the alliance development stage because of too much enthusiasm.

9. Focus. The ability of all partners to focus on the goals and objectives of the alliance is significant. Key here is being realistic about the amount of internal resources each partner can, and is willing to commit to the alliance.

10. Commitment. All the above hinges on the commitment of both upper management and the alliance champions. Upper management must lend full support to the alliance champion in both word and deed. The alliance champion must have the capability (through the support of upper management) to gather the internal resources necessary to make the alliance successful. Through this support comes the confidence the alliance champion will need to achieve the goals and objectives of the alliance.

> *"Somehow I can't believe there are many heights that can't be scaled by a man who knows the secret of making dreams come true. This special secret can be summarized in four C's. They are curiosity, confidence, courage and constancy, and the greatest of these is confidence. When you believe a thing, believe it all the way. Have confidence in your ability to do it right. And work hard to do the best possible job."*
>
> —Walt Disney

Chapter 5

★★★★★★

Pitfalls, Roadblocks & Land Mines

★★★★★★

"We have to distrust each other. It is our only defense against betrayal."

—Tennessee Williams, 1953

"Suspicion on one side breeds suspicion on the other, and new weapons beget counter weapons."

—John F. Kennedy, 1963

Partnering Pitfalls—Caveat Pars

Partnering, as with any activity, has pitfalls and unexpected land mines. While you need to protect yourself from dangerous situations, you do not want to create them by approaching it with the wrong attitude. Conflict, improperly challenged, can be the death sentence to an alliance. Conflict develops in five vital areas: values, goals, facts, procedures, and misinformation. Conflict doesn't have to be a roadblock to a successful alliance if you and your partnering alliance members are willing to resolve the conflict at the core level, in a timely manner. In fact, the resolved conflict can lead to a stronger relationship through improved communication. Unfortunately, conflict that is left unresolved will lead to fatal flaws that will erode the relationship.

Many alliance advocates and consultants believe that the alliance mortality rate is around 50%. If you wait to build partnering relationships until all the potential pitfalls are unearthed, your industry will pass you by: others you might have considered as possible members for strategic alliances might be aligned with your competition. Be realistic though, as with a spouse; partnering alliance members don't change with time. They do not become who and what you want them to be. But rather, evolve to whom and what they desire. If you suspect core problems, you probably are accurate in your assessment and the chance for a successful alliance is greatly diminished. Remember what we said: **Partnering, like marriage, will not change people.** What it does do is to remove the facades and expose the good and bad.

Trust in others and the belief that alliance partnering starts at the top are two elements crucial to your success. These two topics are frequently causes for failed partnering agreements when they're not followed. Also, in alliance agreements, be cautious of things you can't see now but may experience later—little things like the small print in a detailed alliance contract. Don't let your enthusiasm cloud your judgment.

Just because you're working with a company of integrity, it doesn't mean it will look out for you. Even in a partnering relationship, you are still accountable for your own success and well-being. Make sure your bottom-line expectations take into account that servicing the partnering agreement is going to require extra resources. Be certain of everybody's alliance partnering goals. Here are some examples of potential pitfalls—study them before you enter any agreement and your chances for success will greatly increase:

Values

- Partners having conflicting core values involving issues like trust and integrity. Corporate culture clashes, employee turf protection, and resistance of some employees to new ideas can wreak havoc on your alliance efforts.

- One partner not completely embracing the principles of partnering at the top level or even in departments, divisions, or regions while the other does.

- Dupont believes that if a contractor is looking just to maximize his profits, on just one job, then partnering is not for him.

- Because the dynamics of alliance relationships are constantly changing, the inflexibility of partners generally kills an alliance. Each member must *give a little*, especially in times of change, for a partnering agreement to work.

- After making a partnering commitment, a partner may still have a hidden agenda. A partner may decide that they don't want to follow through, or that they do not have the capability to fulfill their commitment.

- Suppliers, when business is great, can make the mistake in the relationship of forgetting the loyalty of their smaller long-term customers and snubbing them for the larger orders. This is short-term profitability and long-term disaster for an alliance.

- Complacency is an insidious relationship-killer. Continuously ask questions in a way that encourages partners to relate problems and shortcomings. Ask, "What haven't we done lately?"

- Dependency on your alliance partner can put your business at risk. If you become the weak link in the alliance, and your alliance no longer delivers value to your partner, they will discontinue the relationship.

- You or your alliance partner is not ultimately relationship-oriented.

- Anger, or blaming others for your current situation, can replace analysis and reason.

- A *not-invented-here* mentality in senior management or a lack of commitment to the alliance and the innovations developed by alliance partners.

- Losing control of a technology or best practice to an alliance partner who becomes a competitor.

Goals

- In situations where a customer is the driving force behind a partnering arrangement, be sure to examine each proposal in the context of your company's overall partnering strategy. This was recently apparent to IBM and they discontinued their alliance with Somerset PowerPC in Austin, TX, and Motorola, in producing microprocessors for Apple.

- When sitting down at the partnering table, a partner might find the partnering seat uncomfortable. It could be that your partner has a different level of emotional and physical comfort, or sometimes the distress can be caused by a change in corporate strategy or a restructuring which leads away from a partner's product and/or technology. Try to understand that underlying need.

- The disloyalty that can occur when you try to partner with a potential or current customer and have them renege on the promise of purchasing from you. There is also the possibility of an unethical partner attempting to capture another's technology or trade secrets. Develop a sense of wariness if you see signs of change.

Facts

- Relinquishing some control with the expectation of greater shared returns can be a difficult waiting game. Additionally, your resources can get pulled in too many directions based on collective alliance decisions.

- Lack of third-party cooperation. All the elemental members of a partnering agreement will have to *"give a little"* for an agreement to work.

- If a partner receives unfavorable media coverage, you are pulled into the picture. Real or perceived, image and reputation are critical to a company's success.

- Contracts with an overseas market, for instance, often take a long time to finalize. By the time you get going, in the technology industries, your competition may have already started.

- Developing an alliance with a partner organization that is weak and bleeding will only bring you down.

Procedures

- Underestimating how much time, energy, and resources will be necessary to commit to your new alliance.

- Culture clashes as with the failed alliances of IBM and Apple. The heralded Fall 1991 announcement promising cooperation eventually spawned Taligent Technology and Kaleida Labs. Unfortunately, the two could not co-exist so the alliances eventually gave way to a quiet winter 1995—1996 breakup.

- In the debris of a failed strategic alliance attempt, your competitor might walk away with your trade secrets or best practices. In the case of the Office Depot and Staples failed merger, Staples learned how Office Depot was beating them in the delivery business. Office Depot's own trucks were delivering orders C.O.D. to small businesses. Later, what did Staples do? That's right. They started delivering small orders C.O.D.

- Not having access to a partner's employees. The closer the planned relationship between the two companies, the greater the importance of the linkages between them.

- A large company partners with a small one. The representatives, usually top executives of the small one, can make decisions on the spot. Unfortunately, employees of most large companies must take a proposal up the chain of command.

- Putting all your alliance relationship eggs in the basket of only one executive or manager. The management tenure of your alliance contact can signal success or failure. Build relationships with several key contacts in the organization of your alliance partner.

- Develop internal reward structure in partnering with customers or suppliers. Traditional reward for buyers come with concessions from the seller and cost reductions. On the flip side, sellers usually offer rewards for sales performance.

- Difficulty communicating across various time zones. Solving problems quickly when your partnering factory is located halfway around the world is hard enough when you speak the same language. Add the increased difficulty of language barriers, and major challenges can emanate from the alliance.

- Inertia. Not having the emotional ownership in getting started.

- Chaos. Seeing too many alliance choices and ways to create an alliance.

Misinformation

- Underestimating the complexity of coordinating and integrating corporate resources, and overestimating your partner's abilities to achieve the end result. Eventually, partnering success depends on management's abilities, skills, commitment, aspirations, and passions in assembling the pieces of the puzzle.

- When unequal dependence in a relationship occurs, the partner with the least dependence is less likely to compromise and put energy into the relationship.

- Different meanings assigned to the same words by different cultures can cause serious problems.

- Unrealistic expectations of any partner's capabilities. These areas include: technology, research, production skills, marketing might, and financial backing.

- Unexpected inefficiencies or poor management practices can be the demise of a well-intended alliance plan.

- Developing an alliance with multiple partners who later become rivals to one another puts a serious strain on the integrity of the alliance.

- Self doubt. Not believing you have the skills and tools to create an alliance.

> *"Lofty words cannot construct an alliance or maintain it; only concrete deeds can do that."*
> —John F. Kennedy, 1963

✔ *Here is an interesting alliance survey tidbit from a sports industry publication, titled* Sportstyle. *They asked retailers and manufacturers questions about why alliances failed. Following are the top responses; Lack of **continuous/responsive attention, planning, leadership** was stated by 80% of the retailers and 64% of the manufacturers. Unequal **contribution/commitment of resources** between partners was stated by 60% of the retailers and 69% of the manufacturers. **Contrast in partner cultures, style or level of trust** was stated by 53% of the retailers and 60% of the manufacturers.*

Now that you've had a view of partnering from the downside, don't let these hurdles stop you. Be clear on what alliance partnering is not. It is not instant gratification, nor is it a quick fix. It is not a flavor-of-the-month management strategy. Strategic alliances are separate entities that have come together to solve their individual problems in a way that serves the whole mutually. It is sharing core competencies that overlap and create synergies. The struggle is a necessary part of any relationship that is valuable and lasting.

> *"Experience is not what happens to a man. It's what a man does with what happens to him."*
> —Aldous Huxley, author, *Brave New World*

Having knowledge of the "alliance unknown" should keep you from becoming immobilized and waiting for opportunities that could easily pass you by. Sure, there are some risks, but to lessen the effects, do your homework, know the agenda of all partners in the relationship, and measure against it. If after doing your homework you're still not completely sold on an alliance relationship with a company, start small. Begin your alliance by partnering with another for a simple or small promotion and get your feet wet.

If you do stumble, having the ability to regenerate after a fall is crucial—especially if you or a partner simply makes a mistake. Be careful when events and circumstances are not what you hoped or planned for. You might go to a place of apathy. If you remain in a toxic mind-set, you will wait for things to get better instead of moving into action. The trouble is that things rarely get better until you propel yourself into a state of activity.

To be successful at partnering you must commit to functioning at a higher level. A level that will allow you to stretch your comfort zone and then commit to moving into action. Without these two issues in concert, you might not get started or restart when necessary. Recently a local doctor heard that one of his patients who had survived one unhappy marriage had married a second time. The doctor remarked that the remarriage was "the triumph of hope over experience." For you to develop an alliance after a failed experience, you too must let hope triumph over your experience.

Once you get back in the action, you can go after small wins to reestablish your confidence to take risks in pursuit of an even larger prize. The key is to not wait for all to be perfect before you commence.

It's okay to *ready, shoot, aim*. Do though, take the time to adjust your aim after you begin. Be like a commercial airline pilot and course correct regularly. Keep your future focus on the partnering journey. Keep it improving. Be decisive, and show the qualities of a leader in your industry. You will be rewarded.

From a Lawyer's Perspective

Curtis E. Sahakian, President of The Corporate Partnering Institute, (800) 948-1700, has given me permission to share with you what he believes, as a lawyer, to be the 12 common partnering mistakes. He works with large corporations in helping to make the road to successful strategic alliances a bit smoother. You too, can receive value from what he shares with the corporate giants.

The Dangerous Dozen Common Partnering Mistakes*

1. Cutting yourself too good a deal. Focus on jointly making money from customers instead of from your partner. It's all too easy to generate grief and bickering if you attempt to do otherwise.

2. Lack of an exit strategy. Whoever best plans for the end of a partnering relationship will best benefit from the partnership.

3. Failure to use deal sheets. A deal sheet is a non-binding outline that walks you, step-by-step through a transaction. One of its key issues is to control your partner's lawyers.

4. Misuse of lawyers. The function served by lawyers is to look after the many details that can turn around and surprise you. You don't want to under use or overuse them.

5. Failure to plan and then keep your eye on the ball. Think through your plan before you start. Determine where you want to go, how you will get there, and what you'll do when you do get there.

6. Negotiating from an ivory tower. You have to communicate with your people. Don't forget to involve and consult with your line managers and technicians. They know things you don't and can't know.

7. Misplaced haste. Attempted shortcuts are more than likely to cause delays or bad deals.

8. Ignoring Details. Details will have a disproportionate impact on the amount of value you capture from a long-term partnership. Make sure you have someone with a firm grasp of the details at the bargaining table and, later, at the helm.

9. Trapping yourself into awkward positions. Making commitments or creating expectations while thinking on your feet can only lead you into trouble.

10. Impairing your ability to "get up and walk." Stay uncommitted until the deal closes. Keep your alternatives open, alive, and in play.

11. Ignoring the foreclosure of other opportunities. Whenever you participate in partnering, you forgo other opportunities. Be aware of what options you may be foreclosing.

12. Wrong deal, wrong partner, wrong reasons. A partnering should leave you continuing to provide your contribution to the value chain that distinguishes you from your competitors.

* Summarized from: *Corporate Partnering: A How-To Handbook, An Executive's Guide to Key Partnering Practices*, The Corporate Partnering Institute

"It's kind of fun to do the impossible."
—Walt Disney

Chapter 6

★★★★★★

Keeping Your Alliance Alive & Healthy

★★★★★★

*"If every fool wore a crown,
we should all be kings."*

—Welsh Proverb

*"Let the sword decide
after stratagem has failed."*

—Arabic Proverb

I have heard it said that in an ideal marriage one partner is blind and the other deaf. There may be some wisdom in this old saying. To keep your strategic alliance alive and healthy, each side must overlook some of its partner's misgivings. This chapter, if you heed the advice, will help you avoid many of the relationship challenges. It will help you keep your alliance relationships on the smooth road to success.

Regardless of how you view the world (the glass is half-full or half-empty), if you enter into a strategic alliance relationship you must focus on survival of the alliance in good times as well as bad. It can be mutually expensive, in cost, time, and emotions to break up an alliance. Your goal is to build **Outrageously Successful Relationships (OSRs)** with your alliance partners. Build relationships that are so successful that neither would ever consider breaking them up.

The Total Value Package (TVP) that you offer your partner, and your partner offers you, is crucial to the alliance success. When you understand what your partner needs and then give it to them, you, in return ,can also ask for extra value. The best way to do this is through regular Relationship Value Updates (RVUs). Quarterly RVUs are preferred, but semi-annually is acceptable if you are serious about building OSRs.

The idea of this is to limit the negative conversations you, or your partner, has about one another when expectations are not met. Unfortunately, unrealistic expectations are common in alliance relationships. Think for just a minute about the worst boss you've ever had. See him (or her) having one of their famous temper tantrums. You know what I'm talking about, when their face turned bright red, and the veins in their neck popped out. See them in your mind's eye. Now! Here's the question, "Is there a chance that this person could have been a decent human being?" Your answer, in the conversation you are having with yourself about them may be "Who knows?" Maybe they were just taught old X Theory management (where one treats their employees like mindless idiots) when they were young, and it stayed with them. Your alliance partner and their organization will have regular conversations with themselves about you and your organization. You can limit the damage and take care of things early with RVUs.

The most effective way to administer RVUs is for you, and your partner, to (hopefully every quarter) complete the RVU, and send it to the other. For alliances of larger organizations and/or with several departments involved, each department should do the same. This will help both sides understand the conversations that their partners are having internally about them. Additionally, when you realize that some of the things you are doing for your partner create high-level value for them and it costs you little, you may be inclined to do more of that thing. Conversely, when you realize that some of the things you are doing for your partner create little value for them and costs you a bundle, you'll quickly cut back in that area.

Relationship Value Update (short form)

1. The value I believe my company has received from our strategic alliance:

_____

_____

_____

2. The value I believe you have received from our strategic alliance:

_____

_____

_____

3. Improvement action steps we plan to take to improve our performance in our alliance relationship:

_____

_____

_____

4. Improvement action steps we would like to see you take to improve our alliance relationship:

_____

_____

_____

Relationship Value Update (long form)

✔ *Check boxes that apply*

1. The value I believe my company has received from our strategic alliance:

❏ Have helped my company's core competency.

❏ Have created valuable synergies for my company.

❏ Have helped us reduce costs.

❏ Have helped us in reducing duplication of effort.

❏ Innovations discovered with your help.

❏ New markets you have helped us to access.

❏ Competitive situations (established and emerging competitors) you have helped us to overcome.

❏ Other valuable benefits we have received.

2. The value I believe you have received from our strategic alliance:

❏ How we have helped your company's core competency.

❏ How we have created valuable synergies for your company.

❏ How we have helped you reduce your costs.

❏ How we have helped you in reducing duplication of effort.

❏ Innovations we have discovered for you and/or helped you with.

❏ New markets we have helped you to access.

❏ Competitive situations (established and emerging competitors) we have helped you to overcome.

❏ Other valuable benefits we have delivered.

3. Improvement action steps we plan to take to improve our performance in our alliance relationship:

_____

_____

_____

4. Improvement action steps we would like to see you take to improve our alliance relationship:

_____

_____

_____

In addition to sharing regular value updates with your alliance partner(s), adhering to a Partnering Code of Conduct will lessen the need for conflict resolution strategies.

Partnering Code of Conduct

1. Be the kind of partner with whom you'd like to partner.

2. Ethics and morals are important.

3. Respect others—their beliefs, customs, and policies.

4. Think as a member of both your alliance and your industry.

5. When in doubt, don't!

Conflict Management & Resolution

In times of conflict you can take one of two positions: first, you can take the position of digging in your heels and believing you are _right_. The second position you can take is the desire to learn, trying to understand what is motivating the other's behavior. My recommendation, as you might have guessed, is the second. Just to make a point, I'd like you to think back to the last argument you had—with your spouse, parent, child, friend, or in a business situation. Do you see yourself in the argument? Now, which position had you taken? The first? The second? If you had taken the position of trying to understand the other's position, there would most likely not have been an argument. We are not perfect, and sometimes we fall into our _stuff_. At these times we are not the best people we could be. But, it is the person who recognizes that they are in their _stuff_, and makes a new behavior decision, that makes a good partner.

You might be thinking, "Thanks for the info, Ed. Why do I have to always be the person who makes the change, the person who makes it works? Why can't it be the other guy once in a while?" My answer to you is simply that you are the one who figured it out first. Get out of your _stuff_ and, as Nike says, JUST DO IT®. Listed below are some additional tactics for your consideration:

- Evaluate your, and your partner's, conflict management styles. Understanding each other is a great start.

- Identify and plan strategies to deal with non-productive behaviors before they crop up.

- Give positive feedback as often as possible so the relationship does not take on a negative tone through only fire fighting interactions.

- Confront problem situations at once rather than waiting for the situation to escalate.

- Invite comments from all stakeholders early in every project, especially your alliance partners.

- Consider using humor, and maybe even humility, in certain situations.

- Encourage dissent at a time and place that serves all involved.

- Review the value of the alliance relationship. Determine how much your circles of interest overlap. Ask if winning this battle will get you closer to an OSR, or further away from it.

- When you hear something you don't like, repeat it back in an informational way. See if the message you received was the same as it was intended. Misunderstanding is the root of much conflict.

- Know your "buttons" and don't allow them to be pushed. You have control in this area.

- Completely listen to what the other guy has to say before you open your mouth. Remember the adage, "Listen twice before speaking once." That's why God gave you two ears and only one mouth.

- Remember the principle of saving face. In some societies, it is a matter of life or death. Fortunately, or unfortunately, depending on how you look at it, this is not usually the situation in North America.

- Keep your ego in check. Be clear on the difference between high self-esteem and high ego. One serves and one does not.

- Appoint a devil's advocate and allow that person to be involved in projects from the start, all the way through completion. Their job is to be a pain in the neck. It's not that they are just picking on a certain person or position. This keeps people from taking a dissenting opinion personally.

- Keep the consequences of your decisions in mind.

- Value the opinion of others. Focus on the clarity of the water, not the spring from which it flows.

Emotional Ownership in Your Alliance

"We know too much and feel too little."
—Bertrand Russell, 1949

Conflict resolution becomes much easier when all the alliance partners have the same emotional ownership in the success of the alliance. Feeling your world and your part in it is quite important in making any type of relationship work. You must be in touch with your intuitive side. But feelings or uncontrolled emotions can be devastating to a successful relationship. Herein lies the challenge: to access important feelings but not let them control you. Rather, you use these powerful emotions to help you achieve what you desire.

"The future belongs to those who believe in the beauty of their dreams."
—Eleanor Roosevelt

"There is one thing stronger than all the armies in the world, and that is an idea whose time has come."
—Victor Hugo

I believe the two previous quotations make the point well for achieving what you want and what is available to you. Unfortunately, many people want, but are unwilling to pay the price. As with everything else, alliance relationships come with a price. I have met many people with fabulous ideas that will never get off the ground. Why? Because they do not have the drive, or as some call it, the "fire in their belly." I'm confident that you, too, have come across this type of person. In contrast, I've met, as you have, people whose ideas are so-so at best. Yet they succeed wonderfully. I believe the reason for the latter's success, is the emotional ownership of their ideas. They have gotten past the doubt and indecision and believe in what they are doing to the core of their being. To make a strategic alliance work, the alliance principles must have this emotional ownership in the success of their alliance.

I told the story in *The Art of Partnering* about Mitsubishi Motor Sales of America in Cerritos, CA and how they tried to change their corporate culture—but after a year of work they had failed. The executives had sent the marching orders to the mid-level managers to make the changes. Then the executives went back to the "more important matters" involved in running the corporation. One year later, nothing had changed. The executives realized that their organization was watching *what they did* and not *what they were saying.* The executives went back and started over, but the big difference this time was that they allowed people at all levels to add to their vision rather than just buy into it. Also, the executives led the charge the second time around. The employees "got it" that the executives had ownership, and that helped the organization experience that same ownership of the changes. One year after their restart, they enjoyed the results. Dan McNamara, VP at Mitsubishi told me that among the improvements, he was happiest with:

- Communications improvement.
- Reduced politics, back-stabbing, and hidden agendas, along with an increased willingness by employees to partner interdepartmentally, keeping others informed.
- Greater productivity through increased creativity and risk taking.

The Journey to Your Emotional Ownership

The path to Emotional Ownership is simple to understand but not as simple to follow. It will help you understand your personal journey to emotional ownership of your ideas, decisions, and dreams. This gut level ownership makes the difference in achieving business and personal successes. Employee or employer, in your business and personal life you continually have challenges. These challenges without solutions or answers will generally cause you to experience extreme pain. To solve or remove this pain, you must move into decisive action. Action delivers solution possibilities for your challenges, thereby removing your pain.

Unfortunately, some people cope by doing nothing. They *hide out* in either denial or substance abuse. Doing nothing is a formula for failure. Doing what you have always done and expecting different results, I call insanity. Nobody intentionally wants to be insane. You can succeed in alliance relationships, and anything else you desire, through understanding your journey to emotional ownership.

Step 1. Idea: Some ideas are gold and some are worthless. You must constantly seek possible solutions to your challenges. Earl Nightingale would sit with a yellow pad thinking of solutions to his day's challenges every morning before the rest of his family awoke. Dr. Robert Schuller's possibility thinking is to list no less than 20 ways to solve your challenge. His 20th is how he started the church that is known today as the Crystal Cathedral.

Step 2. Excitement: When an idea crystallizes, excitement sets in. Your view of the challenge is like a world of possibilities. All is right as you are moving closer to dealing with your challenge and your pain. You start to have a promise of dealing with your challenge and feel success is possible.

Step 3. Hope: From this pinnacle the slow degrade can start. All too often people start backsliding here rather than moving forward. I learned from a speech coach named Ron Arden that hope without how is a hollow promise. This is where hope turns into nope. The reason is that the reality of the challenge is seen as too big, or too hard.

Step 4. Reality: When, in your mind, all there is left is hope without how, a new reality sets in. Without the how or a plan, your conversation with yourself becomes self-defeating. Your new reality becomes that of not understanding or being able to access the knowledge of the steps, work, and pitfalls involved in creating a solution. And now, hopelessness is not far behind.

Step 5. Desperation: Hopelessness leads to desperation. Many people spend their life here. Even people who are moderately successful find it difficult to make a new decision that would position them for greatness. When the pain is at a level so high that anything else must be better, the point of decision is near. But, if you choose to stay here and "hide out" in indecision, failure is sure to follow.

Step 6. Purpose: Clarity of purpose allows you to see and understand the value of your struggle. When you understand what matters to you, you open yourself up to possibilities. The most important possibility is realizing that there is hope when you seek the how. You see the promise of your success through others' successes.

Step 7. Decision: When you know what you are about, the decision to move forward becomes possible. This is where your emotional ownership of an idea or challenge comes alive. No decision, means no ownership, and a continual decline. Yet, with a new decision, solutions appear and your pain starts to diminish. You have now started on the path to emotional ownership.

Step 8. Paying the price and taking risks: This is the emotional ownership truth detector. This is the point on your journey where you must internalize the intellectual ownership of your decision. When you accept that there are prices to pay and you are willing to pay those prices, positive things start to happen. One of the important prices to pay is that of taking risk, this is especially true in developing strategic alliances. As you've heard it said many times before, you must stick your neck out on order to get ahead.

Step 9. Getting help: Relationship building at its finest. Nobody goes it alone. Every successful person seeks help. This is illustrated masterfully is Joseph Campbell's *Power of Myth*. It is part of your hero's journey. Through help from others, innovation becomes possible. The innovation you'll need to solve your challenge and relieve your pain.

Step 10. Accepting Success in your life: Self confidence and self-worth go hand-in-hand. Accepting that you are worthy of success is key. When you have completed your journey to emotional ownership, you do it all over, again and again and again. Additionally, for different situations in your personal and professional life you will find yourself at different places on your journey at different times. Today you may be accepting success in one area while you are in desperation in another and indecision in yet another challenge. It is circular and never ending.

Your Journey to Emotional Ownership

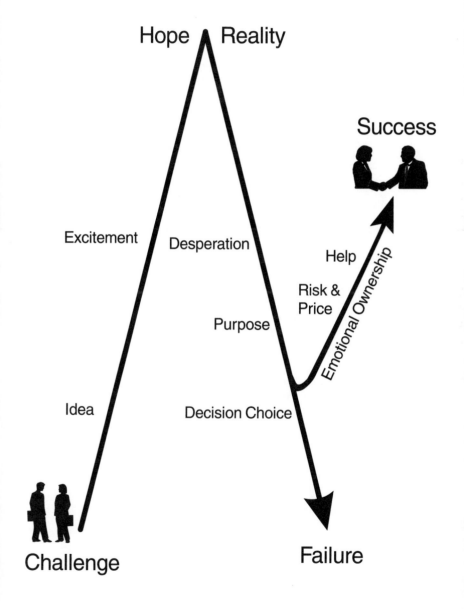

Hope ▲ Reality

Success

Excitement

Desperation

Help

Risk & Price

Purpose

Emotional Ownership

Idea

Decision Choice

Challenge

Failure

Hopefully, this book has helped you in your understanding of the fine art of developing strategic alliances. If developing and maintaining a successful strategic alliance is truly your goal, find your purpose in the idea, make a decision and the emotional ownership will follow. Develop both internal and external **Outrageously Successful Relationships**. As Leonardo da Vinci put it, *"He who is fixed to a star does not change his mind."* Do this, and you are assured successes.

I encourage you to build relationship bridges with those whom you currently work and to those who will follow. I enjoy ending my seminars with this poem by Will Allen Dromgoole, born in 1860. During her father's last summer in the Cumberland foothills of Tennessee, he was 90 years of age. He built a path for her to a stream they enjoyed visiting. Walking the path together, he shared with her his building of the path. Knowing the scant hope of traveling that path with him another summer, she was so moved, she authored this poem. I hope it has as special a meaning to you as it does to me.

THE BRIDGE BUILDER

An old man, going a lone highway,
Came at the evening, cold and gray,
To a chasm, vast and deep and wide,
Through which was flowing a sullen tide.
The old man crossed in the twilight dim,
That sullen stream had no fears for him;
But he turned, when he reached the other side,
And built a bridge to span the tide.
"Old man," said a fellow pilgrim near,
"You are wasting strength in building here.
Your journey will end with the ending Day;
You never again must pass this way.
You have crossed the chasm, deep and wide,
Why build you the bridge at the eventide?"
The builder lifted his old grey head.
"Good friend, in the path I have come," he said,
"There followeth after me today
A youth whose feet must pass this way.
This chasm that has been naught to me
To that fair-haired youth may a pitfall be.
He, too, must cross in the twilight dim;
Good friend, I am building the bridge for him."

Appendix A

★★★★★★

General Issues
Checklists

★★★★★★

The following is a checklist of issues that are common to most types of business agreements. Review it whenever when you put together any type of agreement. If you're like most people, you'll usually find items you overlooked. The checklist starts with legal compliance issues that often apply to Corporate Partnering relationships. It then goes on to deal with specific contractual provisions.

The following checklists are from a lawyer's perspective and shared with you resulting from an alliance with The Corporate Partnering Institute. They are reprinted with permission from Curt Sahakian's *Key Partnering Checklists*. The entire 166-page checklist is available from The Corporate Partnering Institute at (800) 948-1700.

Commonly Overlooked Legal Issues

✔ Do any franchise or business format laws apply? Look for any of the following indicators:

- Use of another's trademark, name, or reputation.

- A required start-up fee or royalty.

- One party's direct or indirect control over the business of the other. Is one party providing a high level of assistance, a marketing plan, or a business format that the other will conform to?

✔ Are you subject to any state dealer termination laws?

✔ Are you subject to any import or trade laws?

✔ Are you subject to any state or federal securities laws?

✔ Are there any antitrust issues that must be dealt with?

- Be especially sensitive to provisions requiring the sale of products at specified prices.

- Are you transacting business with a competitor or potential competitor?

- Is any form of exclusivity being granted or demanded?

✔ Are you subject to any state or federal anti-kickback laws? They can apply to transactions with private companies as well as governmental units.

Commonly Overlooked Tax Issues

✔ What are the tax implications of the transaction?

- Don't overlook any state or province sales or use taxes.

- If the transaction has any foreign or cross border aspects, don't overlook withholding taxes, customs duties, and tariffs.

✔ For each tax, duty, or tariff:

- What is the impact on each party?

- Who pays the applicable taxes?

- Will any of the tax liabilities or benefits be shifted from one party to the other?

- Who bears the risk of a change in tax law?

- Consider stating your understanding of how the tax laws will apply. Then indicate who bears the risk if they deviate from that understanding.

✔ If there is a dispute with a governmental unit over the application of a tax:

- Who decides whether to contest it or acquiesce? Who bears the cost of contesting the tax? Who controls how the dispute is raised?

- Who pays any interest or penalties if the governmental unit prevails?

✔ Transactions with foreigners.

- Transactions between U.S. citizens or companies and foreign citizens or companies are likely to have unusual tax consequences.

    - The nature of these consequences depends on which foreign country or countries are involved and the structure of the transaction.

    - These issues are likely to require specific provisions unique to the particular transaction or relationship.

Commonly Overlooked Pricing Issues

✔ What are the agreed prices?

✔ Does the pricing change over the term of the agreement? If so, on what basis?

- Are pricing changes at the discretion of one party? Are they controlled by a formula?

- Are prices controlled by the consumer price index or some other index?

- Are prices controlled by changes in actual costs? How are these changes determined and verified?

✔ How often can prices be changed?

✔ Is there a ceiling or a floor on price changes?

✔ Are prices affected by increases in the volume of business transacted?

✔ Is there a "most favored nations" or "most favored customer" provision? This is a provision that keeps the pricing (or other terms) at least as favorable as that provided to others.

- You may want to prohibit a vendor who grants you such rights from granting similar rights to other customers because doing so (a) encourages pricing discipline by the vendor, and (b) discourages vigorous negotiation by other customers.

- Note vendors that agree to provide such protection to customers expose themselves to severe margin erosion by selectively targeted lowball bidding from competitors.

✔ Is there a "Last Look" provision (also known as a "Meet the Competition" clause)? This is a provision that provides a vendor the right to keep the business so long as it matches the last best offer of it competitors. This discourages competitors from attempting to compete for the business in the first place.

Different Payment Structure Variations

✔ When are payments to be made?

- Are there any preconditions to payment or any holdbacks until testing or acceptance?

- What initiates an obligation to pay?

  - How much delay in payment is permitted?

  - Is failure to receive an invoice an excuse for non-payment?

✔ Are there late payment fees or interest on late payments?

- When does the interest begin—immediately or after a period of time?

- Is interest calculated back to the date the payment was due?

✔ How are payments to be made:

- Initial deposit followed by payment in full at closing.

- Lump sum, installments, payment with each shipment, delivery, or acceptance.

- Minimum monthly payments.

- What manner of payment is required or what is permitted?

  - Cash, check, certified check, note, wire transfer.

  - Type of currency: Dollars, Pounds, Yen, Marks, Francs, etc.?

  - In what country is payment to be made? At what location is payment to be made?

  - The currency and the place it must be paid can determine who bears the economic burden of foreign withholding tax obligations or currency controls.

- Conditions to payment.

  - Are there any preconditions to payment?

  - Are there any payment holdbacks until testing or inspection of products is complete?

  - Is there any right of off-set or set-off for related or unrelated claims?

✔ Is any credit being extended?

- Is there interest being charged?

- Does the interest rate increase if there is a default?

✔ Changes in payment terms or credit.

- Will there be a right to accelerate some or all payments if any payments are delayed? Is there an acceleration of payments in the event of some other type of default?

- Are there conditions under which payment in advance can be required such as change in credit worthiness?

Types of Audit Rights

✔ Are there any audit rights. Audit rights differ from a right to an accounting.

- With audit rights the auditing party conducts the audit.

- With a "right to an accounting", the audited party is obligated to conduct and pay for a self-audit.

✔ What is the scope of audit rights: financial, technology, contract performance?

✔ Is there a right to inspect and make copies of: books of account, bank statements, documents, records, tax returns?

✔ Does the auditor have the right to use the auditee's photocopying machine? Who pays for photocopying costs?

✔ Who pays the cost of the audit?

- If an audit turns up a shortfall, will this shift the obligation to pay for the audit? How great a shortfall will be necessary? Will there then be an obligation to pay interest, late fees, or a penalty?

✔ Is there an obligation to provide an accountant's letter certifying compliance with payment obligations?

- Must the letter meet specified criteria to be acceptable?

Types of Information Rights

✔ What record keeping obligations do the parties have?

- Obligation to keep complete records.

- Obligation to retain records for a specified period of time.

✔ What rights do the parties have to each other's information?

- Rights to financial statements.

- Rights to obtain copies of income tax filings directly from the IRS. Is there an obligation to make timely annual IRS filings?

- An obligation to automatically furnish reports that are sent to governmental agencies.

- An obligation to automatically furnish all other internally created reports at no cost.

✔ Are there specifically required financial statements?

- Annual, quarterly, or monthly, audited or unaudited, certified by the CFO, accountants management letter.

✔ Who selects the auditing CPA firm? Is there a right to veto the choice? Are there minimum criteria for selection?

✔ Other information rights:

- Annual certification from CFO that the company is not in breach of the agreement.

- A required annual budget and business plan which is subject to approval by specified parties.

- A monthly report explaining significant variances from forecasts and all current developments in staffing, marketing, sales and operations.

- Prompt notice of all lawsuits and regulatory proceedings.

- Copies of all press releases, product announcements, and company newsletters.

- All information concerning discussions or offers related to any type of possible financing or acquisition of the company.

- Notice of any material adverse change in the company's business, assets, intellectual property, prospects, or financial condition.

- Any other information requested about the company.

Different Confidentiality Issues

✔ Is each party obligated to maintain the confidentiality of information disclosed by the other?

- What information is to be kept confidential and what is not?

✔ Is the agreement itself confidential?

- The existence of the agreement, its content, and/or specific portions of the agreement.

- Is there an express right to disclose the agreement to auditors, attorneys, insurance brokers, etc?

✔ What happens if the confidentiality is breached?

Different Exclusivity Variations

✔ Exclusive right to buy from a party. (All you need or all the other party can supply).

✔ Obligation to buy all the output a party is able to produce ("take or pay" or "output" contracts).

✔ Exclusive right to sell to a party all that the party needs. Right to require a party buy all your output.

✔ Obligation to provide all that a buyer requires or needs. Obligation to supply all your output to a party.

✔ Are there any holdbacks such as specific national accounts? Often distributors receive exclusive territories that can not be invaded by third parties but can be poached on by the manufacturer.

✔ Prohibition from selling to or buying from competitors of the other party. Prohibition from selling to or buying from customers of the other party.

✔ Obligation to provide notice of any other selling or purchasing relationships.

Different Ways to Assure Performance

✔ What is the likelihood of the other party becoming insolvent or bankrupt in the near future?

• What if the other party files for bankruptcy and terminates the agreement under protection of federal bankruptcy laws?

• Can the transaction be characterized as a "fraudulent conveyance" or a "voidable preference" under state law or federal bankruptcy laws?

• How difficult would it be for a trustee in bankruptcy to allege, after the fact, that the transaction was one-sided in your favor?

• Could it be alleged that you paid less than 70% of the fair market value of what you purchased? (70% is a rule of thumb followed by most courts)

• Are you a director, officer, or shareholder of the other party? Do you have any other relationship with the other party that might bring the transaction into question?

- Did a director, officer, or shareholder of the other party guarantee the transaction or otherwise indirectly participate in it in?

✔ Personal, spousal, and corporate guarantees. Performance bonds or letters of credit.

✔ Right to terminate the other party's exclusivity if the other party fails to meet required performance levels.

✔ A security interest in tangible or intangible property including future accounts receivable.

✔ The right to retain ownership of product until paid in full.

✔ Money or property placed in escrow (the money or property need not be related to the secured transaction).

- Is the escrow the exclusive source of recourse or is it being used to secure an independent obligation?

- If it is technology (such as plans, schematics, trade secrets, computer software, or documentation):

  - How do you verify when the deposit or deposits have been made?

  - How do you verify that each deposit is the appropriate version or release of the technology and is complete?

  - What rights do you have to the technology once it's released to you?

  - Do you need certain people or expertise to make effective use of the technology? How will you secure the assistance of these people? If these people are bound by confidentiality agreements, do you need waivers of these agreements included in the escrow?

  - Is there any related technology you will need to make effective use of the escrowed technology? How will you secure access to that related technology?

- What triggers the release of the escrow? When is the performance determined to be complete and the escrow terminated?

  - Will portions of the money be released after a period of time? How much time? Will the draw down be staged?

  - Will portions of the money be released upon the occurrence of specific events? What events?

- Escrow operation.
  - Who is the escrow agent and what is the cost of maintaining the escrow? Who pays for it?
  - How are escrowed funds to be invested? Who decides how they are invested? Who benefits from gains or losses? Who must pay income tax on gains until escrow is released?
  - How will disputes over release of the escrow be handled?
    - Is the escrow agent shielded from any liability? What about willful misconduct or negligence?
    - If the parties disagree on the release of the money, what does the escrow agent do? Is the escrow agent entitled or required to wait for a court order resolving the dispute?

✔ Money is held back until performance is complete or otherwise assured.

✔ Detailed product or service specifications, timetables, or other criteria of performance.
  - Are there performance rewards?
  - Are there penalties for deficient performance?

✔ Interest and legal fees on delayed payments.
  - Right to interest if payment is delayed by more than 30 days retroactive to the first day.
  - Right to costs of collection if payment is delayed more than 90 (or 180) days.

Different Types of Remedies

✔ Does the agreement provide for express remedies in the event of its breach?
  - Damages.
  - Compensation for lost profits. Is there a stated formula to calculate lost profits?
  - Right to withhold delivery or stop goods in transit.
  - Right to cover by purchasing substitute goods or services.

- Right to obtain court orders requiring the other party to comply with the agreement.

- Penalties for failing to comply with the agreement (a fixed sum, a formula, or other penalty).

- Right to rescind the transaction and return everyone to their original position.

- Right to correct the other party's default at your own expense and get subsequent reimbursement from the defaulting party.

- Right to accelerate all payments.

- Right to take (or retain) possession and title to specified property. Is there the right to sell the property and retain what is collected?

- Right to terminate an agreement.

- A cross default provision. The breach of one agreement between the parties constitutes the breach of all agreements between those parties.

✔ Are remedies cumulative or non-cumulative? Does the selection of one remedy prevent you from later exercising other remedies?

✔ Are the available remedies limited to what the agreement provides?

✔ Right to withhold payment:

- Until performance is complete or otherwise assured.

- For disputed or unacceptable goods and services.

✔ Is there an obligation to pay for partial performance?

✔ Is a notice of default required before a party is able to exercise its rights?

✔ Operational restrictions on other party until performance is complete:

- Limitations on officer's salaries.

- Requirement to maintain minimum working capital.

- Obligation to maintain specified financial ratios and inventory levels.

- Prohibition of borrowing, lending, or other specified transactions.

- Other restrictions.

✔ Does payment or other performance constitute waiver of claims or acceptance of performance?

Different Right to Cure Variations

✔ Is there a right to cure?

- What types of breaches are curable?

- What types aren't?

✔ How much time, if any, do the parties have to cure a default. Does it vary by type of default or by party?

✔ Is the right to cure lost if there are successive defaults within a specified period of time?

Term of the Agreement—Alternatives

✔ What is the term and how does it change?

- It is a fixed period of months or years?

- Does it automatically renew every period until one party terminates it? Does it continue until both parties agree to terminate it?

- Does either party have an option to extend the term or the agreement? If so do any provisions of the agreement change if it is extended?

- Is it perpetual? Does it take mutual agreement to terminate? This means the other party can't terminate it without your consent.

Termination Issues

✔ Right to terminate the agreement.

- Is there a right to terminate for convenience?

- Is there a right to terminate the agreement by paying a termination fee? The fee can be set in advance or can be determined by a formula.

- Is there a right to replace other party (or seek alternatives), if performance levels don't meet standards?

- What types of breaches or defaults justify termination and what types do not?

✔ Are there standards of performance which affect the term of the agreement?

- A right to renew if certain performance standards are met.

- A right to terminate if certain performance standards aren't met.

- Is there a right to replace other party (or seek alternatives) if performance levels don't meet standards?

✔ Types of performance standards:

- Dollars worth of products, units, percentage of average regional performance of others, national performance of others, measures of quality, timeliness, prompt delivery.

- Sales volume or purchase requirements.

✔ Is time of the essence? Will even a slight delay constitute a material breach?

✔ Is a notice of termination required?

- Under what circumstances must a notice of termination be provided? Under what circumstances is no notice required?

- How much and what type of notice is required before termination?

Condition of Default Issues

✔ What are types of breaches or defaults are most likely to occur?

- Should they be specifically identified in the agreement?

✔ Financial difficulty.

- The company enters bankruptcy or engages in an assignment for the benefit of creditors.

- The appointment of a receiver, trustee in bankruptcy, or similar official for any substantial part of the company's business or assets.

- The company becomes insolvent or becomes unable to meet its obligations as they become due.

- The suspension or termination of business by the company.

- The company deems itself "insecure or unsafe" or fears diminution of value, removal, or waste of subject matter of the agreement.

- The existence of any unappealed judgment that has a material affect on the lessee's financial statements.

✔ Change in ownership, management, or control of the company or a bulk transfer of the company's inventory or assets.

✔ Any attempt to assign or transfer:
  - The agreement.
  - Any other contractual or intangible property rights.
  - Any of the company's inventory or assets.

✔ Violation or breach of the agreement.
  - Any default or material violation of the agreement.
  - Successive defaults of greater than a specified frequency or severity.
  - Failure to make timely payments as required by the agreement.
  - The making of an untrue representation or warranty.
  - Refusals or failure to report information required by the agreement such as sales results.

✔ Occurrence of specified conditions.
  - Withdrawal of either of the parties from specified market areas.
  - Specified changes in applicable laws.
  - The emergence of a new technology or some specific change in market conditions.

✔ Any default under any other related or unrelated agreement.

✔ Miscellaneous.
  - Conduct that causes injury to the other's business reputation or products.
  - Violation of the law by the other party.
  - The terminating party deems itself "insecure or unsafe."

Often Overlooked Post-Termination Issues

✔ Is there a wind down period to permit an orderly transition when the agreement terminates?

✔ Are proprietary rights licensed under the agreement?

- How long do such licensed rights last? Do they last for the term of the licensor's underlying rights?

- Do they continue so long as the licensee continues to pay minimum royalties?

✔ Which provisions survive termination of the agreement?

✔ What are the responsibilities of the parties after termination of the agreement?

- What is each party required to do at the termination of the agreement?

- What is each party entitled to do?

- What is each party prohibited from doing?

- Think— what is it that you would not want to see the other side doing after the agreement ends? What would you want to make sure that the other party will do?

Different Assignment Issues

✔ Is there an express right to assign the agreement (in part or whole)?

✔ If only portions of the agreement are assignable, what are these portions?

✔ Does an assignment require consent of other party?

- Can consent be withheld?

- Are there standards for refusal to provide consent?

✔ Are assignments prohibited?

- Are attempts to assign void?

- Will an attempt to assign automatically terminate the agreement?

✔ Are there pre-conditions to assigning the agreement?

- Prior written notice (specified number of days).

- Payment of an assignment fee.

- Assignor can't be in past or current violation of the agreement.

- Assignee must assume all other related agreements.

- Assignee must meet specified standards.

- Assignor must provide a refundable security deposit.
- Assignor must provide additional assurance of performance: guarantees, performance bonds, letters of credit.

✔ Are there restrictions on what portions of the agreement can be assigned and to whom?

✔ Does a change in ownership or a merger constitute an assignment?

✔ Does the assignor remain liable under the agreement even after the assignment?

- Which rights are assignable and which are not?
- Which obligations must the assignee accept?
- Does the assignor retain responsibility for its obligations?
- Do the assignor's duties under the agreement terminate when the assignee accepts responsibility for them (know as a "novation" of the agreement)?

Different Warranty & Liability Issues

✔ What warranties are included or excluded?

- Product and service types of warranties: commercial practicality, design, fitness for a particular purpose, conformance to regulatory or governmental requirements, performance, manufacturing, materials, merchantability, non-infringement, obtainment of (or obtainability of) government or industry certifications or approvals, quality, results, specifications, title, workmanship.
- Authority: right, power, and authorization to enter the agreement.
- Warranties relating to the status and condition of the other party and its business.
- Warranties related to status and condition of real estate.
- Warranties related to compliance with environmental laws.
- License warranties:
    - Is there a grant of exclusivity? If so, is there a warranty not to directly (or indirectly) interfere with exclusive rights?
    - Warranty of non-infringement and right to grant the license.

- Warranty of what rights remain in the licensor.
- Patent warranties: patentability, utility, validity, enforceability.

✔ Limits on liability (or affirmation of liability).

- Cap on amount of liability. Is the cap on all liability or on specific types of liability?
- Is the cap set at a fixed amount or determined by a formula? Often the cap is the same as the sales price.

✔ Types of liability:

- Contract liability, damage to property, defamation, delays, infringement, lost profits, personal injury, product liability, unfair competition.
- Liability for personal injury or property injury.
- Liability for environmental damages.
- Liability for claims or demands by third parties.
- Liability for false representations made to third parties.
- Consequential damages, exemplary damages, incidental damages, indirect damages, negligence liability, punitive damages, special damages, statutory liability, strict liability, tort liability.
- Liability in instances where vendor has been expressly advised of the possibility of resulting damages.

✔ Are there specific exclusions to the warranties?

✔ Will there be personal certifications by corporate officers that warranties are true and accurate?

✔ Standards of performance: best efforts, commercially reasonable efforts, every effort, material conformance, reasonable efforts, substantial conformance.

Different Ways to Hedge Commitments

✔ Are any of the representations, warranties, conditions, covenants, or indemnifications hedged?

✔ "Best Knowledge" qualifications.

- Representations, warranties, conditions, covenants, and indemnifications are often limited with "best knowledge" qualifications.

- Who's knowledge?

  - The company's, any employee, front line personnel, executive officers, shareholder's?

  - Is it actual knowledge or constructive knowledge (what they know or should know)?

- Is it knowledge after an investigation or without an investigation?

  - What kind of investigation? A reasonable investigation or an investigation meeting some specified level of thoroughness?

  - Who pays for the cost of the investigation?

- When is the knowledge determined, at signing or closing?

✔ Materiality qualifications.

- Many representations, warranties, conditions, covenants, and indemnifications can be hedged by a materiality qualification.

  - It is important where you put a materiality hedge. For example each of the following creates different liability:

  - Warranty of compliance with all material laws.

  - Warranty of material compliance with all laws.

  - Warranty of material compliance with all material laws.

  - Warranty of material compliance with all material laws except for those laws that don't have a materially adverse effect on the business.

✔ Materiality limitations on damages.

- How large must a loss be before it becomes a material loss?

  - Is it unstated?

  - Is it a fixed sum or determined by a formula?

- Materiality limitations can permit "double dipping".

  - You can add a materiality limitation to an indemnification limitation such as a threshold, basket, or cap.

  - Is this acceptable or prohibited?

✔ Anti-sandbag provisions.

- Is one party responsible for a breach of representation or warranty of which the other party was aware?

- If known breaches are not subject to indemnification:

  - Which representations and warranties should be subject to such an exclusion?

  - Who is required to have knowledge of the matter?

  - When is the knowledge determined, at signing or closing?

Indemnification Options and Issues

✔ Are the indemnification rights the exclusive remedy or do they just add to existing rights?

✔ Who are the protected parties (the "indemnitees")?

- The parties to the agreement?

- Directors, officers, shareholders, or lenders?

- Is the indemnification assignable?

- Are protected third parties entitled to independently exercise their right to indemnification?

✔ What other types of damages are specifically included or excluded?

- Direct damages. Related costs such as attorney fees and the cost of investigating and prosecuting claims.

- Indirect losses such as lost profits, loss in corporate valuation, adverse tax impacts, and changes in insurance ratings and costs.

✔ How is the responsibility for indemnification shared among the indemnitors? Is liability joint and several or is it allocated differently among the indemnitors?

✔ How are damages to be measured?

- Will tax benefits be netted out of the indemnification payment? How about insurance payments? What about the time value of money?

✔ Limitations on the amount of liability.

- Is there a "basket", "threshold", or "cushion" on the downside?

- Is there a "cap" or "ceiling" on the upside?

- A "threshold" is a minimum amount of loss that an indemnitee must incur before the it is entitled to reimbursement. Once this minimum is reached, the indemnity goes back to the first dollar of loss.

- A "basket" or "cushion" is similar to a threshold but the indemnitor is entitled only to those loses in excess of the minimum. It's basically a deductible.

- A "cap" or "ceiling" is a maximum amount beyond which the indemnitor isn't liable. Is it a fixed amount or an amount determined by a formula?

- Are thresholds, baskets, cushions, caps, or ceilings applied in multiple combinations? Are they applied differently to different types of liability?

✔ Time limits and survival periods for liability.

- Are there contractual "statues of limitation" that limit the amount of time liabilities will survive?

- Are different liabilities subject to different time limits?

✔ Litigation of the liabilities that are subject to indemnification.

- Does the seller have the right to assume the defense of an indemnified claim?

- Does the buyer have the right to settle an indemnified claim? Does the seller have the right to veto attempts by the buyer to settle claims that are the seller must indemnify?

Appendix B

★★★★★★

Strategic Alliance Resources

★★★★★★

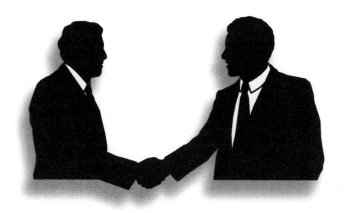

Alliance Works, division of Rigsbee Enterprises, Inc.
P.O. Box 6425-500
Westlake Village, CA 91359
(800) 839-1520
edrigsbee@aol.com
http://www.rigsbee.com

Corporate Partnering Institute
4843 Howard Street
Skokie, IL 60077
(800) 948-1700
(888) 476-9327
cpart@interaccess.com
http://www.corporate-partnering.com

Additional Reading

The Art of Partnering: How to Increase Your Profits and Enjoyment in Business Through Alliance Relationships, Edwin Richard Rigsbee, Debuque: Kendall/Hunt Publishing, 1994

Alliance Advantage: The Art of Creating Value Through Partnering, Yves L. Doz and Gary Hamel, Boston: Harvard Business School Press, 1998

Breakthrough Partnering: Creating a Collective Enterprise Advantage. Patricia L. Moody, New York: John Wiley & Sons, 1995

Business Partnering For Continued Improvement: How to Forge Enduring Alliances Among Employees, Suppliers & Customers. Charles C. Poirier and William F. Houser, San Francisco: Berrett-Koehler, 1993

Can This Partnership Be Saved?, Dr. Peter Wylie and Dr. Mardy Grothe, 1981, out of print

Growth Partnering: How to Build Your Company's Profits by Building Customer Profits, Mack Hanan, 1987, out of print

Intelligent Business Alliances, Larraine D. Segil, New York: Times Books, 1996

Partnering TookKit, Washington DC: NAW/DREF Publications, 1995

Partnerships For Profit: Structuring and Managing Strategic Alliances. Jordan D. Lewis, New York: Free Press, 1990

Sahakian's Due Diligence Checklists, Curt Sahakian, Corporate Partnering Institute, San Diego: 1997

Sahakian's Key Partnering Checklists, Curt Sahakian, Corporate Partnering Institute, San Diego: 1997

The Virtual Corporation: Structuring and Revitalizing the Corporation for the 21st Century, William H. Davidow and Michael S. Malone, New York: Harper Business, 1993